#8 Hitchcock Hall,
Univ. of Chicago.

—

Feb. 1927.

—

ORIGINS OF THE TRIPLE ALLIANCE

University of Virginia
Barbour-Page Foundation

ORIGINS OF THE TRIPLE ALLIANCE

THREE LECTURES

BY

ARCHIBALD CARY COOLIDGE

PROFESSOR OF HISTORY IN HARVARD UNIVERSITY

NEW YORK

CHARLES SCRIBNER'S SONS

1917

PREFACE

In January, 1916, I had the honor and the pleasure of giving the Barbour-Page lectures for that year at the University of Virginia. The substance of those lectures is reproduced in this little volume, though there have been many changes in the form besides the addition of foot-notes. Any one who wishes to understand even in a superficial way the causes that have brought about the present world conflict should familiarize himself with the history of Europe since the Franco-Prussian War, and should try to grasp the interplay of political forces, the aims of statesmen, and the aspirations of peoples during that period. For the greater part of the time the so-called Triple Alliance was the strongest political and military element in the international situation. Its friends declared that it was an element for peace; its enemies regarded it as a conservative league to protect ill-gotten gains. Although it dissolved when brought to the touchstone of actual war, its importance as an international factor for many years makes it well worth our study. In the following three chapters I have tried to point out the causes, personal as well as international, that led to its formation. I have not made any startling discoveries, nor have I new theories to put forth, but I believe I have made use of the best accessible information. Instead of St. Petersburg I ought perhaps to have used the name Petrograd, and I should have done so in speaking of current affairs, but for those of the past it still seems permissible to keep to the older form. For the sake of brevity and smoothness I have often used the word Austria where Austria-Hungary or the Dual Empire would have been more correct; but this, also, is, I think, condoned by current usage.

June, 1917.

ORIGINS OF THE TRIPLE ALLIANCE

THE ORIGINS OF THE TRIPLE ALLIANCE

CHAPTER I

On May 10, 1871, the Peace of Frankfort was signed between the new French republic and the still newer German empire. This date may be regarded as marking, in the conventional way that dates do, the termination not only of a great and dramatic war, but also of a period of European history. With the complete triumph of Germany over France, accompanied by the overthrow of what a few years before had seemed the brilliantly successful government of Napoleon III, with the proclamation at Versailles of William of Prussia as German emperor, with the entry of the Italian troops into Rome, and the ex-

1

tinction of the age-long temporal sovereignty of the Pope, Europe had within
a few months undergone such changes as
to constitute the end of an epoch and
the beginning of a new one. This new
epoch, which closes with the war of 1914,
may be described as that of the ascendancy of Germany.

The Europe of 1871 was represented
and controlled, as it had been for centuries, by certain great powers, jealous
indeed of one another and often in disagreement, but whose collective decision
once reached was in practice binding
upon the rest of the continent. The
composition of the group had varied
from time to time, and the relative
strength and influence of the different
members had been subject to continual
readjustment. They were six in number.
One of them, united Italy, had only just
come into existence and was hardly recognized by the rest as quite an equal.
Imperial Germany, on the other hand,

was a political outgrowth of the kingdom of Prussia, which had been a power for more than a century, and now in its new form, crowned with a halo of victories, it had stepped from the last to the first place among the great European states. Three of the others, Russia, Austria, and France, had been severely defeated in war in the course of the last twenty years, and of these none so disastrously as France.

Ever since the days of Richelieu, for well over two centuries, France had been, with occasional eclipses, the first power in the world. One coalition after another had been necessary to check the ambitions of Louis XIV. The last and most formidable of all, though its armies, led by Marlborough and Eugene, humbled his pride and exhausted his resources, did not succeed in preventing him from seating his grandson on the throne of Spain. Even the fatal reign of Louis XV, with its loss of colonial empires in North

America and India, was marked by the widest supremacy of the French language and of French ideas. Politically, too, France soon began to recover under his successor and enjoyed a partial revenge on England in the war of American independence. Then followed the victories of the Revolution, and the unexampled glories of the Napoleonic empire, when the conquering soldiers of France entered the gates of Berlin and Vienna, of Rome and of Madrid and of Moscow. When at last the tide turned and she was vanquished by combined Europe, only a few years of rest were necessary for her before she again began to assert herself. A generation later, under Napoleon III, she was victorious in the Crimea and in Italy, and once more became the brilliant centre of Europe and the leading power in international affairs.

Now all was changed. France had been overwhelmingly defeated, this time not by a coalition, but by a single foe, in

a war into which she had entered 'with a
light heart' and in which she had lost
every important battle.   A large part of
her territory had been overrun, her capital had been entered by the victorious
enemy, she had had imposed upon her
the payment of an indemnity such as had
never been heard of in history.   She was
deprived of her eastern provinces, Alsace
and part of Lorraine, with some 1,600,000
people, and she was left with a disadvantageous frontier unfortified against a
neighbor who had just given such fearful
evidence of his power.   As a crowning
humiliation, she had to retake Paris itself
from the anarchistic government of the
Commune amid wild scenes of bloodshed,
and this under the very eyes of the Germans.   In the midst of these disasters
she met with little compassion from the
outside world.   Sympathy is the last
thing a vanquished nation may expect to
find, especially if it has excited envy in
the past.   Instead, it is assured that it

has merited its fate by its faults, which are pointed out to it with unsparing frankness.

When we add to all this the fact that in 1871 the government of France was confessedly only provisional, and the existing republican form did not appear to satisfy the wishes of the majority of the people, though there was no telling just what they did want, and finally when we remember that her birth rate had long been declining and was lower than that of any other country in Europe, we can see reason enough for the widespread belief that her sun had set and that henceforth she must content herself with a secondary place among nations. In any event, it was hard to conceive that she could ever again be the first state on the continent.

History records with admiration the way in which the French people and their rulers met and overcame the innumerable difficulties that beset them, and in a surprisingly short time brought order out of

chaos. Their most immediate and pressing task was the payment of the war indemnity, in order to obtain liberation of
French territory from the burden and
shame of foreign occupation. The huge
sums necessary for the purpose were
raised with a promptness that astonished
the world, and made the Germans regret
that they had not insisted on obtaining
more. Then followed the painful process
of recovery from the wounds inflicted by
the war, the arduous work of reconstruc-
tion, and especially the reconstitution of
the military strength of the country.
Not only did the building of a new chain
of fortresses on the exposed frontier cost
by itself many hundred million francs,
but the army had to be reorganized and
reënforced from top to bottom. Here,
too, the progress was soon such as to provoke disquiet, not to say irritation, on the
part of the watchful neighbor to the east.

The question as to the final form of the
government of France remained open for

some years, but in the meanwhile the republicans, at first a minority in the nation and a still smaller one among its leading men, steadily gained ground. The Conservatives, even after they had brought about the fall of President Thiers, were too divided among themselves to profit by the majority they had in the chambers, and in the end, against their wills, they voted a republican constitution.

These circumstances imperatively demanded that the energies of France should be devoted to internal affairs. In consequence, the foreign policy of the third republic was at first cautious, not to say timorous, in the extreme, being dominated by fear of Germany and by the necessity of avoiding complications of all kinds until the country should have recovered its strength. This was no time for France to take the initiative in international questions, or, indeed, to do much of anything, except keep on good terms with other powers, and, if she could not make friends, at least avoid giving offence.

Her Latin sister, the young kingdom of Italy, was equally timid. Italian unity had been achieved in large part thanks to the assistance of stronger nations, and thanks also to their quarrels with one another. The coping stone of the edifice, the acquisition of Rome as a capital, had only been possible owing to the withdrawal of the French army of occupation after the first Prussian victories. This passing of the Eternal City from the hands of the papacy, which had ruled it for so many centuries, had created a painful impression in the Catholic world. It was, indeed, no secret that not only in Austria and Germany, but also among the Conservatives in France, there were not a few who openly advocated the restoration of the temporal authority of the Pope, and were willing to use force to bring this about. The fear of such intervention was for many years a controlling element in Italian foreign policy, and combined with a sense of the weakness and the backwardness of the new kingdom to make its statesmen eminently cautious. The Italians still professed their gratitude for the aid France had given them on the field of battle, but they were disposed to claim that she had repaid herself by her annexation of Nice and Savoy, an act which they still resented. They had not forgotten the French occupation of Rome, and they feared the advent to power of the clerical party in Paris. They were also beginning to entertain ambitions of a Mediterranean empire, ambitions which could not fail to bring them some day into disagreement if not actual collision with their former benefactor. Austria they regarded as a one-time hated oppressor, who still held Italians under her rule, and was capable at any moment of again menacing Italian unity and independence.

Of the great European powers, England was the one that had been least affected by the recent convulsions on the continent; indeed, her position in the world had long been subject to fewer variations than that of others. In the course of the last four hundred years, though often at war, she had met with but one serious defeat, the war of American independence. Even then, heavy as her losses had been, they had brought little direct gain to her rivals. England had never dominated Europe, but she had always been a power of the first rank which continental statesmen could not safely leave out of account, though they sometimes affected to do so. She had reached her highest point relatively in 1815, after her triumph over Napoleon, whom she had opposed so long, often single-handed. In Nelson she had possessed perhaps the greatest of all admirals, in Wellington she had the one general who had been uniformly victorious over the French, and it was her troops that had borne the brunt of the fray in the crowning victory of Waterloo. At that time she was not only the first but in fact the only great maritime and colonial power; indeed, Britannia ruled the waves more completely then than ever before or since. In mechanical invention, too, and in industrial progress, she led mankind.

Since those days, however, her prestige and political influence had somewhat waned. It was not that Great Britain had not made satisfactory progress. On the contrary, in population, in industrial development, in commerce, in wealth, she had advanced without halt, and she had added steadily to her vast colonial empire. Nevertheless, her position in the world, if imposing, was no longer commanding. Although she still held the first place economically, other nations also had modern industries and extensive seagoing commerce. The British navy was still the strongest in existence, but France

and the United States possessed powerful
fleets.   British troops had won many victories over Orientals and savages, but
such successes have never made much
impression on foreign military opinion,
and in the Crimean war, the one struggle
where the English had had to face European opponents, though they fought with
their usual bravery, they did not display
equal competence, and in the later stages
they were completely cast into the shade
by the superior achievements of their
French allies.   Not many people, even in
England, remember the name of the English general in command when Sebastopol
fell.   On the continent there was a tendency to depreciate the British army, and
to regard it as something good enough
against enemies of inferior civilization,
but not the equal of troops trained to
meet more scientific foes.

In the ten years preceding 1871, England had several times been on the verge
of war with other great powers—with the

United States over the Trent affair and over the question of the Confederate cruisers, with Russia over the Polish insurrection of 1863, and with the German states over the Schleswig-Holstein question. In the Trent affair, the demand of England had been acceded to, but in the other cases she had suffered some humiliation. She was still harassed by the question of the Alabama claims, which, as later arbitrated, ended in a triumph for the United States; she had encouraged the Polish revolt by joint diplomatic intervention with France in its behalf, but as she was unwilling to go to the point of war, she had to submit to being severely snubbed by Russia, while the Poles were in the end left worse off than ever; and in the question of Schleswig-Holstein, she had likewise failed altogether to make good her words by action. Of late, especially since the disappearance from the scene of the bumptious figure of Lord Palmerston, the foreign policy of England had been unaggressive and inclined to mind its own business.

During the Franco-Prussian war English public opinion had been in the main favorable to the Germans. This was not due to any especial love for them, though there was much respect for Prussia, but Englishmen had sympathized with the achievement of German unity, and for some years they had disliked and distrusted their former ally, Emperor Napoleon III. The way, too, in which the war had apparently been brought about had prejudiced many against France, as had Bismarck's timely revelations of French desires for the acquisition of Belgium. The first victories of the German armies were, therefore, generally applauded. It is true that, after the overthrow of the Second Empire, the heroic efforts of France to retrieve her desperate fortunes and the severity of the terms of peace imposed upon her produced a certain reaction in her favor, but, as a whole,

English feeling toward the new German empire was one of cordiality and frank admiration. There seemed to be no important matters about which the interests of the two peoples were likely to conflict, and the relations between the two courts were intimate. Prince Albert of Saxe-Coburg, the beloved husband of Queen Victoria, had been a patriotic German, and their daughter was now married to Crown Prince Frederick, the heir to the new imperial throne.

The only power which England viewed with suspicion and hostility was Russia; indeed, there had been little improvement in the relations between the two countries since the Crimean war. The events connected with the Polish insurrection, the renewal of Russian activity in Asia, and particularly the repudiation by Russia of the article in the Treaty of Paris that limited her freedom of action in the Black Sea, had aroused British anger and deepened British distrust of a state whose de-

signs were deemed to be full of menace
to the interests of the British empire.

Russia under Tsar Alexander II had
profited by the bitter experiences of the
Crimean war to put her house in order.
Public opinion, from the emperor down,
had realized that the country was in
need of drastic changes, and that all reforms must be based on the fundamental
one of the abolition of serfdom. This,
perhaps the greatest legislative act in the
history of mankind, had been formally
proclaimed on March 3, 1861. It had
been carried out with the enthusiastic
support of all that was best in the nation
and had been followed up by the insti-
tution of provincial councils and by other
measures of far-reaching importance that
should help to create a new Russia. But,
as was inevitable in a work of such mag-
nitude, there had been numerous mistakes in matters of detail, and the first
enthusiasm of the public was succeeded
by disappointment. The government,

too, alarmed at some of the results of its own policy, had of late grown reactionary, and had thereby aroused increasing discontent among the liberal elements of society. In her absorption in the work of internal regeneration and also in that of reconstituting her military strength, Russia had for fifteen years withdrawn from active participation in international questions. She had taken no share in the events that led to the liberation of Italy and to the unification of Germany. She had, it is true, watched with lively satisfaction the defeat and humiliation of Austria, whose ungrateful hostility at the time of the Crimean war she had not forgiven. For a while she had seemed to seek closer relations with France, but the threat of French intervention during the Polish insurrection, in contrast with the ostentatious friendship of Prussia at this juncture, had led to a reawakening of Russian nationalism and thrown Alexander II into the embrace of his kinsman in Berlin. The Tsar had not only drunk to the success of German arms at the time of the Franco-Prussian war, he had likewise made no secret of the intention of Russia to intervene in case Austria should ally herself to France. In return, Russia, with the complicity of Bismarck, had profited by the French disasters to abrogate the Black Sea clause in the Treaty of Paris in defiance of England and Austria, who had protested angrily, but in the end could only sanction* what they were unable to prevent. In 1871 official relations between Berlin and St. Petersburg were of the most cordial nature, and personal ones were closer still. To be sure, the former friendship of the two chancellors, Gorchakov and Bismarck, had cooled down in the course of time—neither of the two was sentimental in such matters—but real ties of affection bound together Tsar Alexander and his uncle, Kaiser William.

* At the London Conference in 1871.

Austria-Hungary had within a few years undergone profound changes, both external and internal. When Francis Joseph had come to the throne on December 2, 1848, his territories were in the throes of revolutions that threatened the very existence of his empire. Thanks, however, to able generals and ministers, and still more thanks to the assistance of Russia, he had triumphed over Italians, Hungarians, and other insurgents, and had been able to resume his absolute authority. The German Confederation was reëstablished, with Austria once more as its leading member, and presently Russia, an all too powerful friend, was defeated in the Crimean war, while Austria took the opportunity to "astonish the world by her ingratitude." But this period of success had been short-lived. In 1859, Austria had been expelled by the French from Italy, save for the Trentino and the province of Venetia, and had been forced to tolerate the growth of a united Italian state. Seven years later, by the battle of Sadowa, she lost Venetia, and had also to submit to being excluded from Germany, to which her own German territories had belonged by race and history ever since they had come into existence. Her system of centralized despotic rule had now broken down, and disaffection was rife throughout the empire.

It was high time for a change of policy. The imperial government turned to the strongest of the discontented elements, the Hungarians, and offered to meet their wishes. In the negotiations that ensued the Hungarian leaders showed themselves much the shrewder of the two parties. The agreement reached, the so-called *Ausgleich*, was highly favorable to them, for they succeeded in obtaining not only a liberal constitution for their kingdom, but a complete ascendancy for the Magyar race over all other elements in it, and a reincorporation in it of the province of Croatia, thus dividing and weakening the

South Slavs. Hungary, though the less populous of the two halves of the monarchy, was granted equal rights with Austria in every respect, except in the language of the army, and she soon obtained and has kept more than an equal influence in the management of foreign affairs. The least statesmanlike part of the new constitution was the provision that the *Ausgleich* should hold good only for periods of ten years at a time, and should then be renewed by fresh agreement. It is in human nature that such renewals can only be reached after sharp bargaining, and that every ten years the Dual Empire is threatened with a crisis.

Just before the outbreak of the Franco-Prussian war, Austria had been in negotiation with France for an alliance that should bring her revenge against Prussia. The plan had come to nothing, owing to the opposition of the Hungarians, the attitude of Russia, and the sudden completeness of the German victories. Austria quickly saw the error of her ways, and was anxious for reconciliation with her old rival and recently triumphant foe.

All that France had lost in the disastrous war of 1870, and more, Germany had gained. The position of Napoleon III at the height of his fortunes had never approached that attained by his victorious adversary, William of Prussia, now German emperor. The rank of the Germans as one of the great peoples of Europe had long been secure. Their achievements in many fields ever since they had overthrown the Roman empire had assured them a foremost place in the history of the world, and though after the close of their period of splendid accomplishments in the middle ages they had lost their political eminence, they had given repeated proof of their vitality and genius. During the last hundred years they had gained fresh distinction in many fields of human endeavor. German literature could show names that rivalled any in the literature of England or of France; German music had surpassed the glory of the Italian; German philosophy, with its cluster of celebrities of the first rank, had not been equalled since the days of ancient Greece; German science had already come to be regarded as second to none; German universities, as the models of learning and advanced thought, were attracting students from all over the civilized world. Even German military prestige, somewhat tarnished with time, had received fresh lustre from the exploits of Frederick the Great. Since his day, however, it had hardly gained, for Waterloo, where the English had done most of the fighting, did not more than efface the memories of Jena, and the Germans as a whole had the reputation of being not so much a people of soldiers as of thinkers and poets.

In one respect Germany had been for centuries a conspicuous failure. Her people, though not devoid of national feeling and pride, had long seemed unable to form

any real political union. Her magnificent
empire of the middle ages had disinte-
grated into a mass of disjointed frag-
ments, many of them ridiculously small,
and tempting to the cupidity of their
neighbors. The wars of the French Revolution had, indeed, swept most of these
petty states into the melting-pot, and the
final rising against Napoleon had taken
on the character of a true national movement, but the hopes of patriots had been
bitterly disappointed after the overthrow
of the oppressor. Left to themselves,
that is to say, to their governments, the
Germans had been able only to produce
a confederation helpless for any effective
purpose, and one whose two chief members watched each other with constant
jealousy and seldom combined except to
put pressure on the others. The story
of the abortive risings of 1848, and the
lamentable fiasco of the Parliament of
Frankfort appeared to set the seal on
German political incapacity.

Now all was changed. Prussia in six years had fought three successful wars. The first of these, it is true, had been against so weak a foe that it could bring but little glory, but in the second Austria had been defeated in six weeks, and in the third two great French armies had been forced to surrender, others had been repeatedly defeated, Paris had had to yield to a siege, and at Versailles, in the halls that had witnessed the splendors of Louis XIV, there had been proclaimed a new German empire, which seemed to reconcile the conflicting claims of the autonomy of the smaller states and of the necessary predominance of Prussia, the principle of a strong monarchical authority and a modern parliament based on universal suffrage. The political achievement was as remarkable as the military. No wonder that the world was filled with astonishment and admiration. "Europe," it was said, "has lost a mistress and got a master." * Not only was the

* Morley's *Gladstone*, ii, p. 357.

victorious German army without question the most powerful in existence and
under the command of the first general in
Europe, but the destinies of the new empire were directed by the great statesman
who had forged it 'with blood and iron,'
Prince Otto von Bismarck.

In 1871, the German chancellor was
fifty-six years of age. Though somewhat
fatigued by his labors, he was at the
height of his extraordinary intellectual
powers. Since the days of the first Napoleon, no man in Europe had been so
feared and admired. Even his enemies—
and he had many of them—did not venture to question his genius. His dominant personality, his gift of caustic expression, the apparent reckless frankness,
nay, the very brutality of his utterances,
fascinated and subjugated those with
whom he came into contact. Born for
strife, he passionately resented opposition, and was a good hater who seldom
forgot an injury. The difficulties he had
to overcome in winning over his master

to his opinions—for William of Hohenzollern, who took a serious view of his
rights and duties as a sovereign, was not
easy to convince—and the resistance that
he not infrequently met with at the hands
of the parties in the Reichstag, or of the
military authorities, or of hostile influences at court, at times so irritated Bismarck's nerves as to menace a breakdown
of his health and render intercourse with
him difficult. Ever and anon he would
threaten to resign; but, except at certain
critical moments, we may question the
seriousness of his intention. His master,
though sometimes angry enough with
him, recognized the immense services that
he had rendered, and had no thought of
letting him go.

Like other statesmen of the first rank,
Bismarck followed in the main a simple
policy, even if his contemporaries could
not be expected to realize this. He was
infinitely resourceful in detail, keeping
open various possibilities and ready to

change on the instant, if need be, from
one course of action to another; he was
never off his guard, and was constantly
puzzling and bewildering his opponents;
but at bottom his aims and ambitions
were not complicated. Now that German unity had been achieved in the form
he desired, with Prussian supremacy and
the exclusion of Austria, now that France
had been defeated and deprived of her
German territories, he regarded his creation as complete. Henceforth it was not
his object to add to the stately fabric he
had erected. He confined himself to
strengthening it and to putting it in a
position to weather future storms. He
strove to consolidate the new empire, to
make its inhabitants feel its advantages,
to win over the discontented elements, to
stimulate its economic development, to
keep up its military strength at the highest point of efficiency, but there is no
proof that he seriously harbored designs
of further extending its borders. Here

we have one of his remarkable character-
istics. In spite of successes sufficient to
turn the coolest head, his ambitions remained what they had been, and in spite
of the aggressiveness of his manner and
the roughness, if need be, of his means,
he was essentially a moderate as well as
a conservative. The most famous proof
of this in his career was his single-handed
opposition to the desire of the king and
of the whole Prussian army to exact territory from Austria after the victory of
Sadowa. By a desperate effort he had triumphed, and his countrymen have since
been unanimous in recognizing the extraordinary wisdom of his views on this
occasion. Toward France he did not display and could not be expected to display
the same moderation, but he had serious
doubts as to the advisability of taking the
French part of Lorraine. In this case he
yielded to the arguments of the military
authorities, perhaps thinking that as
France would be irreconcilable anyway,

it was needless to try to conciliate her.
Even admitting that his imagination may
occasionally have played with the possibility of fresh conquests,* the policy he
followed in his later years was one of
peace. As a statesman he belonged to
the school of Frederick the Great and of
Talleyrand, not to that of Napoleon. He
lacked, indeed, a certain kind of imagination, and this sometimes prevented his
understanding the forces opposed to him.
Thus in the famous *Kulturkampf*, which
was soon to break out, he long failed to
grasp the real strength of the modern

* Beust, *Aus drei Viertel-Jahrhunderten*, ii, pp. 480, 481. (At
Gastein, August, 1871): "We also spoke of the German provinces of Austria, and Prince Bismarck strongly disclaimed any
desire of acquiring these provinces for the German Empire. . . . I do not question the sincerity of these objections,
but I cannot forget another circumstance in connection with
this subject. 'I would rather,' Bismarck told me, 'annex
Holland to Germany.' When I entered, some months later,
on my post as ambassador in London, the new Dutch ambassador, with whom I had formerly been acquainted, arrived
at the same time. He had hitherto been ambassador in
Berlin. The first thing he told me was that Bismarck had
reassured him as to the rumor that Germany wished to annex
Holland, by saying that he would greatly prefer the German
provinces of Austria."

Catholic church. When he did make the discovery, he extricated himself with his usual skill from a situation that had grown too difficult. In spite of brave words, he ended by going to Canossa, but he did not do so until he had assured himself of a very different reception from Henry IV's, and of picking up a good many advantages from the journey. Though a conservative and an aristocrat, he took the initiative in legislation to ameliorate the condition of the laboring classes, and set an example to Europe for measures of state socialism; but he regarded the socialists themselves with the most narrow-minded intolerance. Geographically, his outlook was limited, reaching little beyond the European continent. Even England he never completely understood, and he looked on the Eastern Question as one that did not touch Germany directly and that, therefore, she should keep out of. For lands farther away he cared nothing at all. Great as he was, he was not in his visions ahead of his times; indeed, if anything, he rather lagged behind them. He had treated the Great Germany idea of 1848 as a foolish Utopia, and he never foresaw that the generation after his own would come to feel that the German unity he had founded was not complete when it left twenty million Germans outside of its domain. Nor did he realize that the industrial development of the empire which he favored and stimulated, breaking a few years later with his liberal supporters and turning from Free Trade to Protection, would with its vast increase of German commerce and shipping lead to the building up of a large navy. He believed such a navy to be a useless and dangerous luxury. In his old age he yielded to a public opinion that had gone beyond him, and entered upon a policy of the acquisition of German colonies, but although in the diplomatic controversies to which his action gave rise he held his own with his accustomed skill and aggressiveness, he had no ambition for a colonial empire; he only cared for trading-posts, and he grudged expense even for them.

In 1871 the relations of Germany with the other European powers were in the main satisfactory. England Bismarck did not like, and he resented British influence at the German court, as represented particularly by the Crown Princess of Prussia. In discussions with England his tone was frequently sharp rather than conciliatory, and he regarded her as being too much interested in her commerce and in her colonial affairs, and too unreliable under democratic influences, to be a state that could be counted upon. At the same time he did not feel that her interests were antagonistic to those of Germany, and would have deemed a serious quarrel with her to be unnecessary and foolish. With Russia Germany was on intimate terms, even if the personal relations between the two chancellors were perhaps not quite so friendly as they once had been. With Austria the first steps to a reconciliation had already been taken; with Italy there was no cause for dispute. The one land whose enmity must be accepted as a permanent fact and appreciated accordingly was France.

With his usual sound judgment, Prince Bismarck realized that France could not be expected to forgive and forget the war of 1870. Her loss in prestige and position were in themselves hard enough for a proud nation to bear, though time might heal the ordinary wounds of the conflict, including in this case the payment of a huge war indemnity. But the loss of Alsace-Lorraine was not a thing that a people like the French could accept as final, at least for a generation, and as long as it was not accepted there would always be Frenchmen who would wish to seize the first favorable opportunity for a *guerre de revanche*. This being so, Bismarck wasted no time in laments or illusions, but faced the situation and shaped his plans accordingly. He was willing, when it suited his purposes, to assume a polite, nay, even a benevolent, attitude toward France, though often his tone was much the reverse, but as she was always a possible enemy, his policy was in the first place to keep her weak and occupied with home affairs, and in the second to keep her isolated.

With these objects in view, he favored for France a republic as the form of government that would suit him best. Court circles in Berlin, like the rest of aristocratic and conservative Europe, would have preferred to see a Bourbon or an Orleans prince restored to the French throne, but such sentimentality did not affect Bismarck. He believed that a French republic would be weak and probably distracted, therefore not in a position to desire a war, still less to carry one on successfully, whereas a prince, whether a Bourbon or an Orleans or a Bonaparte, would feel the need of strengthening his position by gaining the prestige which only a successful war could give him. Undeterred, therefore, by court influences, the chancellor showed himself friendly toward the French republicans, and he even seems to have had a liking for his old acquaintance, President Thiers. When the German ambassador in Paris, Count Harry von Arnim, attempted a policy of his own not in accordance with the prescribed one, he was recalled from his post, tried on a charge of retaining state papers in his own possession, and his career was blasted.

But there was a still stronger reason why Bismarck wished to see a republican government in France. He was convinced that a republic would find it much more difficult than a monarchy to secure alliances with the other great states of the continent, all of which were monarchies. As against France alone, the German empire bade fair to be able hence-

forth to hold its own.   It was already the
stronger power of the two, and, owing to
the difference in birth rate, the disparity
between them would become steadily
greater.   What he feared was an anti-
German coalition, and almost any combination of this kind appeared to him
conceivable.   To the world at large such
a danger might appear remote enough.
The German empire was not only so formidable that no other country would
lightly dream of attacking it, it was also
on better terms with the others than was
its weak, distracted neighbor.   But this
was not enough for Bismarck.   Some
years later, in answer to the charge, "You
have the nightmare of coalitions," he said,
"Yes, necessarily." *   He remembered
that even the genius of Frederick the
Great would not have sufficed to save
Prussia in the Seven Years' war but for
the timely death of the most dangerous

* Conversation with Count P. Shuvalov. *Gedanken und
Erinnerungen*, ii, p. 224.

of the king's enemies, the Empress Elizabeth. And a new alliance of these same powers—Russia, Austria, and France—that had so nearly brought Prussia to destruction in the eighteenth century, was not unthinkable against Germany in the nineteenth. Nor was this the only peril. In 1870 Austria and Italy had both been disposed to draw the sword against Prussia. A little more diplomatic skill and willingness to make concessions on the part of Napoleon III, or a French victory or two at the outset of the war, might well have led to a triple alliance with which even the armies of von Moltke would have found it difficult to cope, except, perhaps, with Russian assistance, an assistance that would have had to be paid for some day. It was true that since Germany had triumphed, Austria and Italy had hastened to express their friendliness and to put far from them all thoughts of hostility. Bismarck's old antagonist, Count Beust, was now anxious to be his friend. But the chancellor had a good memory, and he looked further ahead than the mere present, however glorious. The friends of today had been the enemies of yesterday, and might be the enemies of tomorrow. No precautions could be too great in such vital matters. At the time these fears appeared without foundation, but the events of recent years have shown their extraordinary foresight.

The policy of Bismarck, accordingly, was to keep France isolated by every means at his command, both direct and indirect. Whether he happened to be on bad terms with the government at Paris and addressing it in a menacing tone, or whether he seemed indifferent and openly contemptuous, or whether he was just then conciliatory and willing to do favors, he never relaxed in his efforts to prevent the republic from finding an ally in any other great power. Circumstances aided him, and as long as he remained at the helm, France did not succeed in emerging from her isolation.

The obvious way for Germany to avoid all danger of a hostile coalition was to become, herself, a member of some alliance so strong that it would have nothing to fear from any number of foes. In the memory of men then living, there had been a league which, after it had overthrown the Corsican conqueror of Europe, had dominated the continent and had maintained law and order often by the mere terror of its name and the knowledge of the immense forces at its disposal. The union of Russia, Austria, and Prussia, given a mystical consecration in 1815 by the so-called Holy Alliance, had lasted for more than a generation. There had been occasional friction between its members, and even an interruption of good relations in 1829, owing to divergences over the Eastern Question, but the Revolution of 1830 in Paris had brought the three conservative powers together once more, and they lived in substantial harmony until the outbreak of the Crimean war. Since that event, to be sure, intercourse between Austria and Russia had been devoid of cordiality, and Prussia and Austria had actually fought against one another in 1866, but first Russia and then Austria had had her lesson and had learned by it. In the defeat and humiliation of Austria, Russia had her revenge for Austrian ingratitude, which she was now willing to forget. Austria, on her part, after her own disasters and that of France, was in a somewhat perilous position, in view of the permanent ill will of Italy and the close friendship between Berlin and St. Petersburg. The counsel of wisdom suggested that she should break with the past, and, frankly accepting her present situation, should forgive and forget whatever grievances she had entertained against her two former partners. Instead, therefore, of showing resentment when the new empire was proclaimed at Versailles,

Austria gave assurances of her entire satisfaction and of her desire to be on the best of terms with the Germany to which she had ceased to belong.

This was what Bismarck wanted, and he now reaped the reward for his moderation in 1866. No other combination possessed such attractions for him as the binding together of the old allies into a new League of the Three Emperors. For, as long as this league should last, French schemes of a *revanche* would be innocuous. It would represent, too, not merely a vast military force, but, as in the past, a grouping of the conservatives of Europe. And Bismarck, like his master, was thoroughly conservative. He had never at heart renounced the principles which as a Prussian *Junker* he had proudly defended in his early days. Even if he had more than once made use of revolutionary forces when they suited his purposes and had accepted universal suffrage as part of the foundations of the new German empire, to the great realist these were but means to his ends, and he used them without scruple when convenient. None the less, he remained a conservative. He could maintain good relations with republics, nay, he preferred one in France, but his natural friends were the champions of the altar and the throne, the long-established guardians of law and order, the governments that ruled their people, not those that were ruled by them.* It seemed wise, too, in view of the recent alarming growth of international socialism, for the conservative powers of Europe to forget their dissensions and once more emphasize the solidarity of their permanent interests.

On August 11, 1871, at Ischl in Austria, the German emperor paid a visit to Emperor Francis Joseph. A few days later their chancellors, Prince Bismarck and Count Beust, came together in conference and discussed the relations of the

* *Gedanken und Erinnerungen*, ii, p. 229.

two empires, and interchanged expressions of mutual good will. But the feud between the two men in the past had been too bitter for them to have any real confidence in one another. It was only when Beust, the Saxon, had been succeeded as foreign minister for the Dual Empire by Andrássy, the Magyar, that intimate relations became possible between the Ballplatz and Wilhelmstrasse. In his earlier years, Count Julius Andrássy had been officially hanged in effigy as a rebel and traitor. He was now the representative of the triumph of Hungary as well as of the new direction of Austrian policy. In 1870, when Hungarian prime minister, he had strongly opposed Austrian participation in the war between Prussia and France. He was also on good personal terms with Bismarck. We have it on his own authority that from the start he aimed at obtaining for Austria admission as a third party into the intimacy that existed between Russia and Germany,

and then at the gradual supplanting of
Russia in German good graces.*

But even before the fall of Beust, the
next step had been taken toward drawing together the two empires. On September 7 Emperor Francis Joseph returned at Salzburg the visit that had been
paid him at Ischl. Etiquette demanded
that the next visit should be paid by the
Austrian emperor in Germany, and policy
required that it should be in Berlin, the
capital now not only of William the
Prussian king, but of William the German emperor. This public tribute to the
new empire of his Hohenzollern rival
must have cost not a little to the pride of
the heir of the Hapsburgs, whose house
had so long borne the imperial crown.
But whatever the sacrifice was, Francis
Joseph resolved to make it. Friendly relations could be had on no other terms.
It was arranged, therefore, that he should
come to Berlin in state, accompanied by

* Wertheimer, *Graf Julius Andrássy*, iii, p. 226.

his new foreign minister, who had already had a meeting with Bismarck.

The news of the intended visit may well have awakened some apprehension and jealousy at St. Petersburg, as perhaps foreshadowing a change in Prussian, now German, policy. At any rate, it was not for the interest of Russia to see herself supplanted at Berlin in her position of best friend. For this or for other reasons, Tsar Alexander, when informed officially of what was to take place, asked: "Why am I not wanted, too?"* Of course, there could be but one answer, and with all speed he was sent a cordial invitation.

From the 5th to the 11th of September, 1872, the three emperors and their foreign ministers met in the German capital amid high festival, while Europe looked on and wondered what might be the intent

* The Tsar was urged to take this step in a confidential letter he received from his former German teacher, Schneider. It is possible that Bismarck instigated the letter.

and the scope of their conversations. These conversations resulted in a general agreement, but the entente thus concluded did not take the form of a written alliance. The sovereigns and their ministers, instead of formal conferences, held a number of separate interviews, during which they exchanged expressions of good will and assurances of mutual support. They also explained their policies to one another and made clear that there was nothing in the intentions of any one of them to which the others might fairly object. The attitude of Austria was naturally more reserved than that of Russia and of Germany, for she was in the position of a former enemy just admitted to the society of two old friends.* Nevertheless, the Austrians had no cause for complaint in the way they were received, and they were, or fancied they were, the objects of more popular acclamation than the Russians.†

* Broglie, *La Mission de M. de Gontaut-Biron*, p. 45.
† Wertheimer, ii, p. 77.

The old league of the three great conservative European states was thus re-
constituted, more powerful, more imposing, than ever. Again it dominated the
continent. Not only was the combined
strength of its armies incomparably superior to any force that could be brought
against them, but as long as it lasted each
of its members could feel safe against attack by land. But there was one very
important new feature to the league.
The relative position of the three allies
had changed profoundly since the days
they had first gone hand in hand with
each other. When, in 1815, Tsar Alexander I had formed the Holy Alliance,
there was no doubt that he was its most
powerful sovereign and leading spirit,
even if in subsequent years he came under
the influence of the Austrian chancellor,
Prince Metternich. In the time of Nicholas I the primacy of Russia was clearer
still, so much so that after 1849 Austria
and Prussia were almost in a dependent
position. Prussia, indeed, had through-

out been the weakest of the three allies, a docile follower of the other two; she had never taken the lead in their joint policy.

In 1872 the situation in this respect was different. It was evident to the whole world that the mightiest of the three empires was that of Germany and the first of their statesmen was the German chancellor. It was Germany that had brought together the other two members of the league, and it was in Berlin that the general reconciliation had been effected. Whatever else this renewal of former intimacies might mean, it meant without question one more brilliant achievement for the policy of Prince Bismarck.

The next few months served to strengthen his position even more. In May, 1873, together with his sovereign and with von Moltke, he paid a visit to St. Petersburg, where he found many old acquaintances from his days as Prussian minister there eleven years before. He now came as the lion of the hour, entertained and run after by all the highest society of the city. In return he had no hesitation in recognizing the debt that he and his country owed to Russia, and is said to have declared before his departure: "Si j'admettais seulement la pensée d'être jamais hostile à l'Empereur et à la Russie, je me considérerais comme un traître." * His master went even further and concluded a treaty of alliance with Alexander II, which was countersigned by the two field-marshals, von Moltke and Bariatinski, but to which Bismarck refused to append his signature, giving as his excuse that he objected to "binding conventions in circumstances where there was as yet no positive object in view." † Almost immediately after the departure of their German guests, Tsar Alexander and Prince Gorchakov went by invitation to visit the Vienna Exhibition of 1873. Fresh expressions of good will

* Tatishchev, *Alexander II*, ii, p. 100.
† Moritz Busch, *Bismarck, some Secret Pages*, ii, pp. 480, 481.

were exchanged, matters of common interest were discussed in the most amicable
spirit, and an agreement was concluded
which may be regarded as a counterpart
of the one between Russia and Germany
at St. Petersburg.* Emperor William,
also, in his turn came to Vienna, and another distinguished guest appeared in the
person of Victor Emmanuel, king of the
Italy so long bitterly hostile to Austria,
and so recently united at her expense.
His visit showed at least a desire to establish better relations between the two
states; and as he followed it up with one
to Berlin, where he met with a cordial
reception, the Italian kingdom seemed to
be following in the orbit of the three empires. Great Britain, though unenthusi-
astic, was friendly; France could only
look on, lonely and helpless.

The diplomatic triumph of Bismarck
was thus complete, and he could have little to fear from any foreign quarter. At

* Wertheimer, ii, p. 89.

home, on the other hand, matters were not going to his taste, for he was in the thick of a struggle with the Catholic church, the so-called *Kulturkampf*, a conflict into which he had entered without realizing the enormous latent power of his adversary. The more deeply he became involved, the worse became the difficulties that it brought upon him, and the less the prospect of a satisfactory issue. This told upon his nerves. He was also much irritated by the opposition he encountered in various other quarters, and he especially resented the intrigues, real or imaginary, spun against him by the Empress Augusta and her friends. His health, as well as his temper, was affected by all this; so that he more than once threatened to resign, and perhaps seriously thought of doing so.

Meanwhile the rapid recovery of France had first astonished and then angered and alarmed the Germans. The French had paid off their tremendous war indemnity with unexpected facility; and now that their territory was evacuated by the enemy, they were building up, in spite of the storms of their internal politics, a new army on a firmer basis and a larger scale than ever before. This army was intended primarily for purposes of defence —French policy in those days was nothing if not timid—and it was still no match for that of Germany. Nevertheless, this too rapid recuperation awakened displeasure and anxiety, especially among the German military authorities, who were inclined to argue that, however peaceful the intentions of France might be for the moment, yet, as she had not abandoned the hope of getting back Alsace-Lorraine, she would profit by the first favorable opportunity to undertake a war of revenge. Granting that such was the case, would it not be wise for Germany to provoke a conflict now, before France had recovered her full strength or had found an ally, and then, after defeating her a second time, to impose upon her terms that would render her harmless for the future ? Such reasoning was not unnatural, and there is little question that both at this time and later several of the military leaders, including von Moltke himself, desired another war. On the other hand, there is no ground for thinking that the emperor had any intentions of the sort. He wished to end his days in peace. Bismarck's position is not so clear. Several times in his memoirs and elsewhere he expressed his disapproval of 'preventive wars.' On some other occasions his tone was different.*

Early in 1875, Europe was startled by a sudden war scare, an episode whose true significance has not been entirely cleared up to the present day. In February

---

* *Denkwürdigkeiten des Fürsten Hohenlohe-Schillingsfürst,* ii, p. 107 (February 18, 1874): "Bismarck: 'We want to keep the peace; but if France goes on arming so that she is to be ready in five years, and bent on war at the end of that time, then we will declare war in three years.' This he had told them quite plainly."

Count von Radowitz, one of the trusted
servants of the chancellor, and newly
appointed minister to Greece, was despatched on a special mission to St. Petersburg. According to Bismarck's un-
convincing later explanation, he was sent
to straighten out certain matters in the
machinery of the diplomatic relations
between the two capitals. It has been
charged, however, and there is reason for
believing, that the real object of the mission was to obtain for Germany, in return
for a promise of support in the Eastern
Question, a free hand from Russia in case
of war against France, but that this object
was not attained. At any rate, the
French foreign minister, the Duc Decazes, was disturbed, and on March 11
communicated his fears to Lord Lyons,
the British ambassador in Paris.* On the
following day the French Chamber voted
a bill which had been under consideration
for some time, to add a fourth battalion

* Lord Newton, *Lord Lyons*, ii, p. 68.

to each regiment. It was in vain that France declared that her intentions were purely defensive and that she was not materially increasing her armament; public opinion in Germany was inclined to regard the measure as a menacing if not hostile act. On the 8th of April the Berlin *Post*, a newspaper supposed to be on good terms with the authorities, published a violent article entitled "War in Sight." Three days later the article was reproduced without contradiction by the *North German Gazette*, which, as was well known, was often inspired by the foreign office. The French government now felt serious alarm, an alarm which was heightened by the report of the Duc de Gontaut-Biron, ambassador in Berlin, that in conversation with him at a banquet, von Radowitz had discussed the ethics of 'preventive wars' and had expressed the opinion that Germany would be justified on grounds of humanity as well as of policy in beginning hostilities with France instead of

waiting until France had recovered
enough strength to attack with better
prospect of success. Bismarck later declared that Radowitz carried his wine
badly and was in the habit of talking non-
sense after a banquet, but in view of the
strict discipline the chancellor kept among
his subordinates, it is unlikely that one of
them would venture so far on his own
authority, and there is no sign that Radowitz was ever reproved for his loquacity
on this occasion. Nor were his remarks
the only ones to cause anxiety. Reports
came in from several quarters of menacing
language held by Bismarck, by Moltke,
and by German diplomats at foreign
courts. On May 5 Prince Hohenlohe,
ambassador at Paris, made a formal communication to the Duc Decazes that 'the
German government was not entirely
convinced of the inoffensive character
of the French armaments,' and that
'the German general staff considers war
against Germany as the ultimate object

of those armaments, and so looks forward to their consequences.'* The chancellor was feeling just then particularly harassed by various difficulties that beset him, and on this account, or as a tactical move and means of pressure, on May 4 he asked permission of the emperor to retire from office to take care of his shattered health. The permission was not granted, and was hardly meant to be.

Meanwhile the French had wasted no time, but had appealed for support in pressing terms at both London and St. Petersburg. On April 15 General LeFlô, their ambassador in St. Petersburg, had communicated his fears and those of his government to the Tsar, who had reassured him and declared that during a visit he was about to make to Berlin he would clear up everything. England, too, promised to add her influence to that of Russia to check any hostile designs on the

---

* A. Dreux, *Dernières années de l'ambassade en Allemagne de M. de Gontaut-Biron*, pp. 108, 109.

part of Bismarck.   On May 6 the London
Times startled the world by an article,
based on information secretly furnished
by the Duc Decazes, which revealed to
the public the gravity of the crisis.   The
storm, however, soon blew over.   On
May 10 Alexander II and Gorchakov arrived in Berlin.   When the Tsar took up
the matter, Emperor William declared
emphatically that he had no thought of
war with France.   Bismarck, too, treated
the whole affair as a newspaper excitement and a plot on the part of his enemies to discredit him, but he had to submit to being lectured by Gorchakov, and
had also to listen to official exhortations
from the British ambassador.   He was
not the man to relish such a lesson, and
he was further exasperated by a diplomatic circular of Gorchakov announcing
that "peace is now assured," a bit of
needless vanity which Bismarck never
forgave.

The whole incident of the 'war scare of

1875' remains mysterious. Most German writers have accepted Bismarck's assurances on the subject. Many Frenchmen and some other foreigners have accused him of having planned mischief, but of having been foiled by the intervention of Russia and England.* We may well believe that Emperor William was innocent of warlike intentions at this time, but the chancellor was capable of creating a situation which would force his master's hand. He may have been feeling the pulse of France for his own purposes without having made up his mind as to his future course of action; he may merely have intended to browbeat her; he may, perhaps, as was feared in Paris, have thought of sending an ultimatum demanding a reduction of French armaments, a demand which the French were determined

---

* Sir Charles Dilke, an unusually well informed and competent observer, declared a dozen years later: "There can be no doubt that . . . in 1875, when Russia prevented a war between Germany and France, and England took credit for having done so, Germany could have crushed her rival." —*Present Position of European Politics*, p. 37.

to refuse at all risks, and which they would have regarded as tantamount to a declaration of war. The truth will probably never be known with certainty. What is certain is that at London and St. Petersburg (though not at Vienna, which maintained an attitude of reserve) both the sovereigns* and their ministers, after first treating French alarms as groundless, became convinced that there was serious reason for anxiety and acted accordingly. Even some persons in Germany entertained the same fear, among them the Crown Prince.†

Matters soon settled down, and in outward appearance the League of the Three Emperors was unaffected by what had passed. In reality, the effects were lasting, especially upon Prince Bismarck. To begin with, it had been made clear to him that in case of another Franco-Ger-

---

* After the incident was closed, Queen Victoria had some correspondence with Emperor William on the subject.

† Mrs. Wemyss, *Memoirs and Letters of Sir Robert Morier*, ii, p. 350.

man war Germany could not count again
on the moral support or even the inaction
of Russia.   Friendly as Alexander II was
to Germany, it was, after all, plainly
against the interest of Russia that France
should once more be crushed and still
further weakened. The Tsar had now
shown that he understood this and wished
to maintain the existence of France as a
great power, however inconvenient such
an existence might be to Germany.   Secondly, Bismarck was not the man to forget a bad turn and still less a humiliation.
From now on he bore a grudge against
his former friend, Prince Gorchakov.

As long as no serious conflict of interest
arose between the three imperial partners
in the League, some divergency of views
and the personal pique of their ministers
might not be of consequence.*   But who

* Sir Robert Morier, after seeing Gorchakov at Wildbad in
June, wrote (*Memoirs*, ii, p. 362): "It is clear that in the
'happy family' of the three Kaisers, each of the 'mutual
friends' is endeavoring to convince the public that he has
an exclusive monopoly of the affections of No. 3."

could tell when such a conflict might arise? There was one domain where jealousy between Russia and Austria dated back to the early years of the eighteenth century, where there was always at least latent antagonism between them, and where every disturbance of the status quo at once threatened to bring their interests into sharp collision. Twice before in the last fifty years the alliance of the conservative powers had been disrupted by the affairs of Turkey, and now once more, in the summer of 1875, came the news that a rising had occurred in the Turkish province of Herzegovina, and that Europe must again face the incalculable difficulties and dangers inseparable from a reopening of the Eastern Question.

CHAPTER II

The Eastern Question, that cause of such perplexities to statesmen and of so much bloodshed among peoples, may be said to have begun with the beginning of European history. The story of the hostility between Europe and Asia, and of the struggles for predominance in the lands of the eastern Mediterranean, can be traced back in the first pages of Herodotus to the semi-mythical piratical expeditions that culminated in the Trojan war, and it can be followed down through the ages to the conflict between Austria and Serbia in 1914, which has involved in its gigantic extension one-half the population of the world.

In the course of the centuries the tide of conquest has surged to and fro. Persia invaded Europe but was beaten back; Europe, as represented by Alexander of

Macedon and later by Rome, overran and subdued western Asia, which, with North Africa, became part of Europe in history and culture and remained so for many generations. With the rise of Islam the reaction set in. In the seventh century the Arabs won back Syria and North Africa to Asia, and subjugated Spain and even a part of France. In the eleventh, the Seljuk Turks broke the power of the Byzantine empire and conquered Asia Minor. In the fourteenth, the Ottoman Turks crossed into Europe, and by the middle of the sixteenth they had built up a dominion reaching from the Persian Gulf almost to the Strait of Gibraltar and up into the borders of Austria.

Then the tide turned once more. The Turks, after a last great offensive movement, which brought their hosts in 1683 to the walls of Vienna, met with defeat there at the hands of the Polish king, John Sobieski. This disaster was quickly followed by others, and by the time of the

Peace of Passarowitz, in 1718, after another calamitous war with Austria, the
Ottoman empire from being a terror to
its neighbors bade fair to become their
prey. Already, two centuries ago, people were talking of its extinction in
Europe as a likely event of the near
future.

With the decline of the power of the
Turks, which has continued with little
interruption to the present day, and has
been marked by oft-repeated loss of territory, the Eastern Question entered into
a new phase. It has not been confined to
the relations between them and the various claimants to their heritage. The relations of those claimants to one another
have played an equal and often greater
part. By an extraordinary historical co-
incidence, the years in which the Turks
were first being defeated and shorn of
lands they were never to regain, witnessed
also the sudden appearance upon the
scene of European politics of a new state

destined henceforth to be a perpetual
menace to them. A few months before
the siege and deliverance of Vienna, Peter
the Great had ascended the throne of
Russia. When he came to manhood his
first important act was to wrest from the
Turks the port of Azov and obtain access
to the waters of the Black Sea. Ever
since then Russia, which under the iron
hand of Peter assumed at least the outward semblance of a European state provided with a modern governmental ma-
chine and army and diplomatic service,
has taken a foremost part in the affairs of
the Near East. But she has not had the
field to herself. She has from the first
met not only foes but rivals, and her chief
rival has been Austria. Little as they
have liked it, Russia and Austria, in all
their calculations and plans in regard to
Turkey and later to the Christian states
of the Balkans, have had to take each
other into account for the last two hundred years. Their ambitions and inter-

ests have continually come into conflict,
and the two powers have been often
enough on the verge of war with one another. It is, in truth, a remarkable fact,
that, critical as the situation has been between them, jealous as they have shown
themselves of one another, they have
never actually come to blows until the
world conflict of 1914.*

The almost permanent hostility between Russia and Turkey, who are at war
with one another for the tenth time, has
been based on causes historical, religious,
social, and economic. The Turk has been
the successor of the Tartars, the former
masters of the Russians, who even at the
time of Peter the Great as Turkish vassals held the whole territory north of the
Black Sea. The Turk has been the infi-
del, the Asiatic, under whose tyranny
millions of Christians, the Orthodox
brethren of the Russians and many of

* The nominal hostilities between them on two occasions
during the Napoleonic period can hardly be termed war.

them fellow Slavs, have groaned and suffered for centuries. The Russians on their part have regarded their country as the successor and avenger of the Byzantine empire, destined to erect the cross once more on the cathedral of St. Sophia, and to liberate Greek Orthodox Christendom, and especially the oppressed Balkan Slavs, from Paynim rule. As the population of Russia has increased, it has expanded southward into the prairie lands, richer and more fertile than the northern forests, but it has only been able to make its way by driving back the Tartar and the Turk. Even yet it has not reached open water. In order to gain access to western Europe, the great and growing maritime commerce of the regions north and east of the Black Sea must pass through channels still in foreign hands. Russia has grown to greatness largely at the expense of the Turks, and it seems impossible that she should have permanently good relations with them as long as the entrance to the Black Sea remains under their control. Again and again the Eastern Question has been the chief of her interests. She has often not known her own mind; she has made her fair share of costly blunders; but, in the main, her policy has been consistent, and has been dictated, though at times unconsciously, by natural laws as well as by the sympathies of her people. Only occasionally and for short intervals has she posed as the friend and defender of the Turk.

The chief disadvantage with which Russia has had to contend has been the distances that her forces have had to traverse before they could arrive at the scene of action. They have had to operate from remote bases and to overcome one line of defence after another. But these drawbacks have diminished as her frontiers and her settled territory have been pushed farther to the south and her means of communication have improved. On the other hand, the fact that her

people have been of the same faith and
of the same race as the majority of the
Christians of European Turkey has given
to her conflicts with the Ottoman empire
a moral justification and a popular national character of the utmost value.
They have been crusades and wars of
liberation. In recent years, as fanati-
cism has declined, the religious sentiment
has been replaced by an almost equally
potent nationalistic one. The desire to
aid brother Slavs rather than brother
Orthodox has fired the Russian popular
mind, but the effects have been much the
same, and have strengthened, and, indeed, more than once forced, the hand
of the government of St. Petersburg.

Conversely, Russia, as the one independent and mighty Orthodox power,
was long looked upon by most of the
Christian subjects of the Sultan as their
protector and future liberator. Their
hopes and their sympathies have turned
naturally to her, not to Catholic Austria,

the zealous daughter of the hated Roman
church. Russia could count on these
Christians for such assistance as they
could give in furnishing her with information, aiding her agents, and smoothing the
way for her armies. Even of late, when
the religious motive has receded into the
background, the Russians, though they
have lost most of their hold on the Rumanians and Greeks, have been in a much
better position to win over the Montenegrins, Serbians, and Bulgarians, their
fellow Slavs, than have the Germans and
Magyars of Austria-Hungary. It has
also, for the same reasons, been easier for
Russia than for Austria to stir up troubles
in the dominions of the Sultan or to find
causes for interfering in behalf of his oppressed subjects. The rôle of defender
of the oppressed has, indeed, never been
a peculiarly Austrian one.

The situation and policy of Austria
have been widely different. Until 1870
the government at Vienna was usually

more concerned with the affairs of Germany and of Italy than with those of the Ottoman empire. It has been consistent in its determination that Russia should not be allowed to dispose of affairs in the East without consulting the interests of Austria, but it has more than once changed its mind as to whether those interests could better be served by protecting the Turks against Russian aggression or by a division of Turkish spoils. In the eighteenth century Austria usually leaned to the latter policy. Since then, for the last one hundred and twenty years, she has been for the most part the friend of the Ottoman empire, though not a sentimental one, and quite ready to profit at its expense if that should seem the wisest course. She has had the strategical advantage of being near to the scene of action and of occupying a position which threatened the exposed flank and long line of communication of the Russian armies when they had advanced far to the southward.

With the early years of the nineteenth century a new element appears in the Eastern Question. The Christian subject nationalities, which for generations had submitted passively to Turkish rule, began to reassert their rights to independent existence and to strive to cast off the yoke of the oppressor. With these movements the Russian people ardently sympathized from the first, and the government of St. Petersburg also supported them, though rather intermittently. Austria, on the other hand, cared nothing for the wrongs or for the aspirations of Greeks and Serbs and Rumanians, whom she regarded as clients of Russia, nor did she wish to see them achieve independence at the expense of her former foe but now convenient neighbor, the Ottoman empire. She, therefore, bitterly opposed the intervention of the powers that led to the liberation of Greece. At the time of the Crimean war, she not only ordered the Russians out of the Rumanian principalities, but after it was certain they were

defeated, practically joined the alliance
against them which forced them to the
Peace of Paris, and by a treaty with England and France guaranteed the integrity
of the Ottoman empire.

That empire, thus set up again by the
powers, enjoyed a few years of progress
and reform, but soon the process of de-
composition set in more rapidly than
ever. Corruption and misgovernment
were everywhere rampant, and the money
wrung from an overtaxed people was
squandered in wanton fashion, until in
1875 the national debt was scaled down
by partial repudiation. Security of life
and property, or justice before the courts,
hardly existed for the Christian subjects
of the Sultan. It is no wonder that they
looked across the borders with envy to
their more fortunate brethren in the little
Balkan states which had succeeded in
emancipating themselves, wholly or in
part, from Turkish rule. It was also in
the nature of things that they found sym-

pathy not only among their free Balkan kinsmen but also farther away, a sympathy heightened by a nationalistic movement that had been going on in the Russian empire itself.

The intense consciousness of nationality which has been so potent a factor in the history of the world since about the beginning of the nineteenth century, even if at bottom much the same everywhere, has taken on many shapes in different countries. In Russia one of its manifestations has been a keen new interest in the fate of the other Slav peoples and a desire for union with them. As a purely sentimental idea, based on real or fancied community of race, language, and culture, but without political objects, this movement has been called Slavophilism. Akin to this, but going a step further, and with the avowed aim of bringing the various Slav peoples into some sort of common political system, has been the better known movement termed Pan-

slavism. Not unnaturally this last doc-
trine was regarded by foreign countries
with Slavic subjects as a menace to their
integrity, especially as it found partisans
among all the Slav peoples. In 1867 their
ideals were set forth with much fervor in
a Panslavic Congress held in Moscow.
Panslavism had by this time obtained no
small hold on Russian public opinion,
and could count its orators and its poets
and its many local societies whose object
was not only to preach the cause but to
give assistance to brother Slavs suffering
under foreign oppression.

The imperial government at first looked
on the movement with little favor. Ever
since the days of Peter the Great the
Russian court and administration had
cared more for being regarded as full-
fledged exponents of general European
civilization than they had for any pecu-
liar virtues of the Slavic race. It was
difficult, too, to harmonize Panslavic
ideals with the severity which had been

meted out to the Poles since the insurrection of 1863.   Nevertheless, the Panslavists had their friends at court and in the official world of St. Petersburg, and were supported by a widespread national feeling.

The Balkan Peninsula presented an obvious field for the activity of those zealous for the cause of Slavic welfare. Serbia and Montenegro had, indeed, won their liberties, but there were still several million Slavs groaning under the evils of Turkish misrule.   It is no wonder that they found ardent sympathy in Russia, and that Panslavist organizations there not only sent them money for schools and for many other needs, but also encouraged their hopes of independence and aided them to plot and prepare for it.   The authorities in St. Petersburg seem to have kept aloof from these activities, though they must have had some cognizance of them; but the able and not too scrupulous ambassador in Constantinople,

Count Ignatiev, an ardent Panslavist, gave ground for English and Austrian accusations that the Russian embassy was a centre of conspiracy against the integrity of the Ottoman empire. In spite of this, Ignatiev had more influence with the Sultan than had any of his colleagues.

The special object of Russian interest was the Bulgarians. They had reawakened to national consciousness later than had the Greeks and the Serbs, but now they were awake. Since the middle of the century there had been an active Bulgarian movement, not outwardly disloyal, yet, in the nature of things, concealing under its efforts for education and progress hopes for political emancipation. It had already achieved one notable success in 1870, when, thanks in part to Russian influence, the Sultan had been persuaded to consent to the establishment of a Bulgarian ecclesiastical exarchate, independent of the Greek patriarch of Constantinople. The action of Russia on this occasion showed that times had changed, that the Greeks were no longer her favorites as in the days of Catherine II, but that in her sentiments toward the Christian populations of the East the nationalistic impulse had now taken the place of the old religious one.

Bad as conditions were in Bulgaria, they were still worse in the territories of Bosnia and Herzegovina. Here the unfortunate Christian peasantry had to suffer not only from the usual exactions of the Turkish official and tax-gatherer, but also from the oppression of the upper classes, a landowning aristocracy who, though of Serbian origin, were Mohammedan in faith, and treated their serfs with brutal harshness. The mountainous nature of the region, which made insurrection easy and its repression difficult, the patent weakness of the Turkish government, and the spectacle of the success of their brethren in Serbia in achieving independence contributed to make a rising of the hard-pressed Christians in Bosnia and Herzegovina an event that might occur at any time.

But here the interests of Austria would at once be vitally affected. Already, in the wars of the eighteenth century, Austrian armies had entered these regions. Since 1815 Bosnia and Herzegovina had been surrounded on three sides by Austro-Hungarian territory, and they formed the obvious hinterland for the maritime province of Dalmatia, which without them had unsatisfactory connection with the rest of the empire. The possibility of their acquisition must have been often in the minds of the statesmen in Vienna, especially since the loss of Venice had weakened the position of Austria in the Adriatic and given her a dangerous rival there in the new kingdom of Italy. The military authorities frankly advocated the annexation of the territory at the earliest favorable opportunity, and there is reason for thinking that the emperor himself was anxious to obtain compensation in this way for the loss of Lombardy and Venetia, and not to go down to history as one of the few Hapsburgs under whose rule the dominions of the house had grown smaller, not larger. In 1875 he paid a visit to Dalmatia with an ostentation and in a manner that seemed to show interest in the land beyond the borders of the province.

When, therefore, in the course of that autumn news began to reach Europe of an insurrection in Herzegovina which soon spread to Bosnia, and which the Turks appeared unable to suppress, there was little to surprise but much to alarm those who cared for the preservation of European peace. However cordial the intercourse might be between Austria and Russia, however specific the political agreements, however friendly the sovereigns, experience had shown again and again that the raising of the Eastern

Question was fraught with danger to good relations between the two empires. Twice before in the nineteenth century it had brought them into sharp opposition to one another, and now at St. Petersburg and at Vienna every one knew that the League of the Three Emperors was too feeble a bond to maintain Austro-Russian harmony if there should be a serious clash of interests.

At first there was little difficulty in maintaining the concert of the powers. All of them were sincerely anxious that the conflagration that had broken out in the Balkans should not spread farther. The nearest available consular officers were sent to hunt out the insurgents and persuade them to lay down their arms and trust to the promises of the Sultan. This they refused to do; they had lost faith in such promises. As there was no doubt that their grievances were real, and as the sins of the Turkish administration were notorious, the three imperial

governments entered into communication
with one another and agreed upon a note
which took its name from Count Andrássy, and which demanded from the
Porte, besides an armistice, a series of
reforms, including the equality of Christians and Mohammedans, the abolition of
the farming of taxes, an improvement of
agrarian conditions, and the appointment
of a mixed Christian and Mohammedan
commission to look after the carrying out
of these measures. England and France
adhered to this note, and on January 31,
1876, it was presented in Constantinople,
where after some parley it was accepted
in principle by the Turks. But the insurgents were not satisfied. They made
counter-propositions, demanding not only
greater concessions but guarantees; that
is to say, that the powers should see to it
that the Turkish promises were carried
out. The Turks in their turn promptly
refused, and fierce desultory fighting continued, while thousands of refugees fled

into Dalmatia and Montenegro and agitation increased among all the Balkan Slavs. Aroused by this state of affairs, the three imperial governments determined to make another effort. It was agreed that their foreign ministers should meet in Berlin and come to a further decision on Eastern affairs. This time Prince Gorchakov took the lead. He was emphatic in his disbelief in Turkish promises and favored some vigorous step, but met with unwillingness on the part of Andrássy. A new note, however, was drawn up, known as the Berlin Memorandum. The suggestions of the Andrássy note were reiterated, and it was declared that the carrying out of the necessary reforms must be under the safeguard of an international commission. Finally, in case the Turks should remain obstinate, there was a distinct hint at coercion.

Up to this point there had been at least apparent agreement among the great powers. But the League of the Three Emperors had made a mistake in assuming that all the other European states would accede without discussion to whatever decisions were submitted to them. France and Italy might not be in a position to follow an independent course, but Great Britain had just then as its prime minister a man who held lofty ideas about his country and had definite views as to the course he meant to pursue.

Benjamin Disraeli, soon to be made Earl of Beaconsfield, may be termed the first of modern English Imperialists. To him the British empire was no mere abstraction; it was a great world power with interests everywhere and a right to be consulted and listened to everywhere. This right he meant to assert. The coronation in 1876 of Queen Victoria as empress of India was not the bit of empty theatrical display it appeared to many. It was an assertion of the imperial position of the sovereign of Great Britain,

and as such a declaration of policy. Disraeli hardly entertained many illusions
about the Turks; but the Orient had long
appealed to his imagination, and he believed that England could and should
play a great part there. He had already
achieved one brilliant diplomatic success.
By his sudden secret purchase of the Khe-
dive's shares in the Suez Canal he had
strengthened the position of Britain in
the East at the expense of France, who
saw her control of the great waterway,
built by a Frenchman with French money,
slipping away from her, yet could only
look on with impotent chagrin. Toward
Prince Bismarck he seems to have felt at
this time a certain personal dislike, and,
it may be, jealousy, but the real foe, in
his eyes, the power that he ever watched
and distrusted, was Russia. His feelings
in this respect may, as has often been
asserted, have been influenced by his
Jewish origin, but they were in accordance with English traditions of the pre-

vious twenty years, and they were natural in the breast of a statesman who had visions of a splendid future for his own country. At this very time the violently anti-Russian ambassador of Britain at Constantinople was sending home alarming reports of Muscovite intrigue.

When the League of the Three Emperors had agreed upon the Andrássy note, London had acceded, though without enthusiasm. Now when there came a second document on Eastern affairs, concocted without the participation of Great Britain, and merely submitted by telegram with a request for a prompt adhesion, British dignity and the spirit that guided British policy asserted themselves. The reply sent was not prompt, and when it did come it was a flat refusal. "Her Majesty's government appreciate the advantage of concerted action by the powers in all that relates to the questions arising out of the insurrection, but they cannot consent to join in proposals which they do not conscientiously believe likely to effect the pacification which all the powers desire to see attained." *

This put an end to the unanimity of the powers, and also to any impression that the Memorandum might make on the Turks, who now felt that they had, as in 1854, friends on whom they could rely for support, even without following their advice. Meanwhile the situation in the East had become grave, for the excitement among the Christians of the Ottoman empire had stimulated counter-excitement among the Mohammedans. On May 6, 1876, a mob in Salonica murdered the French and German consuls there. On May 29 the stupid and profligate Sultan Abdul-Aziz was overthrown by a revolution. Six days later he was assassinated or committed suicide. He was succeeded by his brother, Murad V, who after a few months was deposed in his turn on account of insanity and re-

* *Parliamentary Papers*, 1876, lxxxiv, Turkey, no. 3, p. 171.

placed by Abdul-Hamid II, then a very young man. In May there were risings in Bulgaria, and in time rumors from there reached Europe of sporadic insurrections followed by fierce repression. On July 1 and 2 Serbia and Montenegro, carried away by their sympathies for their insurgent kinsmen in Bosnia and Herzegovina and by the hope of adding these territories to their own, declared war on Turkey.

As was inevitable, the news of what was happening in the Balkans at once affected Russia. The nation espoused with enthusiasm the cause of the brother Slavs. Gifts of all kinds, and volunteers, including army officers, came pouring into Serbia. Public opinion began to clamor for war, or at least intervention, and the government itself could not, if it would, remain indifferent to the pressure that was being put on it.

It was not, indeed, to be expected that Alexander II and his ministers could sit with folded hands as mere spectators of whatever events might occur in the Balkan Peninsula. Sooner or later they must take some decisive action. Every Russian tradition in the Eastern Question made this imperative. But besides the probable hostility of England, they had, as so often before, to reckon with the attitude of Austria, especially since the immediate cause of the crisis had been the troubles in Bosnia and Herzegovina, the part of the Balkan Peninsula in which she was most interested. It was well known at St. Petersburg that Austria, having abandoned the hope of playing a rôle in German and Italian affairs, was now looking more toward the Ægean, and was not inclined to remain a merely passive spectator. Also, it was at least suspected that she could rely on the good will and perhaps the actual support of Germany. As early as 1867, the Austrian minister at St. Petersburg had suggested that if Russia were to regain Bessarabia,

Austria ought to have Bosnia and Herzegovina. Gorchakov had combated the idea, but not very strenuously.* We do not know whether it was considered again at Berlin in 1872. In the conversations that took place there, Gorchakov and Andrássy agreed not to meddle in the internal affairs of the Ottoman empire, but not to aid it in suppressing insurrections in its dominions, even if appealed to. The first stipulation might be regarded as a concession on the part of Russia, the second on that of Austria, so long the supporter of the status quo. In the following year, when Alexander II visited Francis Joseph in Vienna, the question of Bosnia and Herzegovina seems to have been taken up again and an understanding was reached but not put down in writing. A treaty of alliance, however, of a general nature was concluded at the pal-

* Count Friedrich Revertera. The incident is narrated by him in an article in the *Deutsche Revue* for May, 1904 (pp. 139–140).

ace of Schönbrunn and signed by both sovereigns, who pledged themselves to full confidence in one another and to common action for the maintenance of European peace.* The time had now come when it was urgent to pass from these vague generalities to something more definite,

* Revertera declares that there was a signed agreement that in case of a Russian-Turkish war Austria was to remain neutral, and in case of a Russian victory was to obtain Bosnia and Herzegovina. Russia was to have a free hand in settling the affairs of the other Balkan territories, but must not retain possession of Constantinople and must notify Austria in advance of the terms of peace. This statement cannot be reconciled with the account given by Wertheimer (iii, 89), who had consulted the copy of the compact in Andrássy's own handwriting. Revertera declares that he got his information from one of the Russian diplomats present at the discussion; but, writing about the event many years afterward, he may well have confused previous discussions and oral agreements with what was actually put into written form. According to Wertheimer (ii, 118), quoting from the unpublished correspondence of the German ambassador, Prince Reuss, when Andrássy visited St. Petersburg in 1874, Gorchakov declared to him emphatically that an Austrian occupation of Bosnia and Herzegovina would mean a *casus belli*. On the other hand, the promptitude with which the understanding was reached at Reichstadt would suggest that the terms had been discussed earlier. It is curious that neither Goriainov nor Wertheimer nor any other writer, so far as I know, has alluded to Revertera's article.

especially as divergencies of policy were beginning to manifest themselves.

It was under these circumstances that the emperors of Russia and Austria, accompanied by their foreign ministers, once more met, on July 8, 1876, at the Bohemian castle of Reichstadt. The interview lasted but a few hours and the scant accounts of it that have been published contain several discrepancies. Still, the main outlines of what was stipulated are clear. No official document was signed, but an understanding was reached and noted down, though some of its details may not have been put in writing or even formally expressed. Two hypotheses were discussed: the victory of the Turks and the victory of the Serbians and Montenegrins. In the first event, Russia and Austria were to preserve the two little Christian states from suffering permanent loss. This looked simple, but the second contingency—and it seems to have been regarded as the more probable of the two

—was much harder to provide for. A defeat of the Turks might well mean the end of the Ottoman empire in Europe. In that case, what should be the policy of Russia and Austria?

The arrangement on this subject concluded at Reichstadt showed astonishing moderation or disinterestedness or weakness—call it which we will—on the part of Russia. It provided for a number of slight additions of territory to Montenegro, Serbia, and Greece, and also for an independent Bulgaria and Albania (Constantinople was to be a free city), but there was to be no large Balkan Slav state, whether Serbian or Bulgarian, that could be either a dangerous satellite of Russia or a real obstacle to Austrian progress farther to the southward at some future date. Austria was to have immediate possession of Bosnia and Herzegovina. All that Russia stipulated for herself was the fragment of Bessarabia that had been taken away from her at the Peace of Paris in 1856,* and this, though it gave her a foothold on the lower Danube, was a matter of pride rather than of real importance, and, secondly (but perhaps not in writing), a rectification of her frontier in Asia, a matter in which Austria felt no interest.   No wonder that Emperor Francis Joseph and Count Andrássy are said to have left Reichstadt well satisfied.†

Events in the Balkans now ran their course, but not in the way that had been expected.   The Ottoman state which had shown itself incompetent to put down the insurrection in Bosnia suddenly rallied in the face of new perils.   The feeble risings in Bulgaria had been quenched in the blood of some twelve thousand of the inhabitants, men, women, and children. It is true that the Montenegrins held their own, but the Serbians, whose terri-

---

* But not the islands of the delta, which she had held from 1812 to 1856.

† A. Fournier, *Wie wir zu Bosnien kamen*, p. 23.

tory was soon invaded, were defeated in
one encounter after another, in spite of
the streams of Russian volunteers that
came to their aid.   On August 29, Prince
Milan appealed to the powers for media-
tion.   At the news of these disasters the
excitement in Russia increased, and the
clamor for armed intervention in behalf
of the Balkan Slavs became ever louder.
The government could not but take heed
of this, and, while refusing to allow itself
to be hurried into precipitate action, it
urged the calling of a general European
conference, and even suggested to England that she take the initiative.

The game of political and diplomatic
intrigue was at this moment particularly
intricate.   The League of the Three Emperors still existed, and the relations between the members were in theory close
and cordial, but not one of the partners
had complete trust in the others.   Circumstances beyond their control seemed
to be pushing them toward an estrange-

ment, if not worse. Bismarck, Gorchakov, and Andrássy were all diplomats of more than ordinary skill, and each was now trying to feel his way with the others. Bismarck, the ablest of the three, was also in much the strongest position, for, besides representing the most powerful empire, he had the fewest difficulties at home to contend with, and he had no immediate ambitions to serve or vital interests at stake.

In August General Manteuffel was sent with a letter from Emperor William assuring the Tsar of his undiminished friendship and of his readiness to support him.* Manteuffel also seems, following in the steps of the Radowitz mission of the previous year, to have suggested a new treaty of alliance between Germany and Russia, presumably on the same sort of terms, namely, freedom of action against France in return for support

---

* The language was perhaps stronger than Bismarck approved.

in the Eastern Question. Again Emperor
Alexander refused to entertain the suggestion. Instead he asked that Germany should keep Austria in check.
Matters were not going well between St.
Petersburg and Vienna. Owing to the
Ottoman victories the Reichstadt agreement soon ceased to fit the situation.
Austria no longer showed any zeal for the
betterment of the Turk; she at first refused the conference of the powers when
suggested by England; and though she
later consented to it, she made it clear
that she would not consent to the political
autonomy of Bosnia, or to its annexation
to Serbia. Such an attitude could not
but provoke irritation.

It happened that Alexander II was at
that time at Livadia in the Crimea, as
were a number of the chief Russian generals, who were naturally occupied with
the political situation and with plans for
a possible campaign in the near future.
Suddenly General von Werder, the Ger-

man military representative specially attached to the Tsar, was asked to inquire
by telegraph whether Germany would
remain neutral in case of war between
Russia and Austria. The question was
most unwelcome to Bismarck, who tried
to evade a direct reply; but when it
was repeated with urgency, he at last
answered that Germany could indeed put
up with it that her friends should win
or lose battles against each other, "but
not that one of the two should be so
severely wounded and injured that her
position as an independent great power
taking its place in the councils of Europe
would be endangered."* This was plain
enough. As no one in Russia had any
fear that she might need German support
to maintain her position as an independent great power against Austria, the real
meaning of Bismarck's reply was that
Russia, despite the fact that she had been

* See Bismarck's account of the matter. *Gedanken und
Erinnerungen*, ii, p. 214.

prepared to fight Austria if necessary in behalf of Germany six years earlier, now could not count on German neutrality in a Russo-Austrian war. A couple of weeks later Bismarck once more sounded Gorchakov as to whether, in return for the assistance of Germany in the East, Russia would guarantee to her the possession of Alsace-Lorraine. Again the proposal was declined.*

Baffled in its hope of obtaining a promise of German neutrality in case of a breach with Austria, the government of the Tsar, which was being reluctantly driven toward a Turkish war by popular feeling at home, turned again to its professed ally and friend in Vienna. Already, before von Werder had left Livadia, and before Bismarck's reply had been received, a special envoy had been sent to Emperor Francis Joseph bearing a letter from the Tsar, in which Alexander proposed that in order to put pressure on the

* Wertheimer, iii, p. 249.

Turks the Austrians should occupy Bosnia and Herzegovina, the Russians Bulgaria, and that an allied fleet should be sent to the Dardanelles.

In Vienna these overtures met with a cool reception. Neither Count Andrássy nor his master had the slightest desire to go to war with Turkey. Partnership with Russia was looked at askance by many elements in the Dual Empire, and particularly by the Hungarians, who had Turkish sympathies and who had not forgotten that their revolution in 1849 had been put down by Russian armies. Even the idea of annexing Bosnia and Herzegovina was none too popular, except in military circles. The Germans and the Hungarians, the dominant nationalities in the two parliaments, feared the results of so large an addition to the Slav elements in the population. Andrássy, therefore, found himself in a delicate situation. He does not appear to have been eager for the annexation, and he was anxious, if it should come, to have it come peacefully, but he was determined not to let the territory go to any other power or to permit any new obstacles to be placed in the path if annexation should prove to be desirable. Accordingly, Emperor Francis Joseph, while reserving the rights and interests of Austria whatever might be the outcome of the existing situation, refused to take any joint steps with Russia toward actual coercion of the Turks. A fresh interchange of imperial letters produced no further agreement. In other words, Austria, though admitting that conditions in the Balkan Peninsula were intolerable, was none the less determined to leave the risk and burden of intervention to her ally, and yet to take her full pound of flesh. Who could feel sure that even the friendly neutrality which was all that she offered was to be relied upon, and that when once the armies of her ally had made their way well to the southward, and she could threaten their long exposed line of communications from her dominant position on their flank, she would not come forward with new demands?

Meanwhile, in England the reports of the Bulgarian atrocities, elaborated in a famous pamphlet by Mr. Gladstone, had excited such public indignation as to dampen for a time the pro-Turkish zeal of Lord Beaconsfield's administration. In Russia the war party was temporarily mollified by an ultimatum on October 31, summoning the Porte to grant within forty-eight hours a two months' armistice to Serbia. Even before receiving it the Turks, yielding to English advice and still more to the necessities of the situation, had decided to make the concession. None the less, Russia was steadily preparing for war, and on November 2 the Tsar, in an audience given to Lord Loftus, the British ambassador, while earnestly disclaiming all desire of territorial ag-

grandizement and especially of the acquisition of Constantinople, declared:
"He wished to maintain the European
concert, but if Europe remained passive,
he would be obliged to act alone."* On
the following day he sent a third personal
letter to Emperor Francis Joseph, and
fresh instructions to his own ambassador
at Vienna to negotiate for the friendly
neutrality of Austria even though she
had refused her coöperation.

But now Lord Beaconsfield sounded a
blast. At a Guildhall banquet on November 9 he proclaimed that "though
the policy of England is peace, there is no
country so well prepared for war as our
own," and he continued in a strain which
was generally interpreted as a menace to
Russia. Next day the Tsar replied † in
an address to the nobility at Moscow, in
which he declared that in spite of herself

* *Parliamentary Papers*, 1877, xc, p. 576.
† It is not certain whether he had already received news of
the Guildhall speech.

Russia might have to draw the sword; and on the morrow he emphasized his remarks by an order for the mobilization of six army corps.

The English government, however, had already issued an invitation to the powers for a conference at Constantinople.* The programme was based on the recognition of the integrity of the Ottoman empire and a disclaimer of all individual advantages on the part of the powers, but the object of the meeting was the elaboration of a satisfactory plan of reform and autonomy for the Balkan Christians. Lord Derby suggested peace and the status quo for Serbia and Montenegro, autonomy for Bosnia and Herzegovina, and guarantees for an improved administration of Bulgaria. Russia was in sympathy with these proposals. Austria was not; but as she could not make public the real grounds for her objections to the auton-

* We may attribute this to the foreign secretary, Lord Derby, rather than to the premier.

omy of Bosnia and Herzegovina, she obtained a definition that it was local administrative reform, not political autonomy, that was meant; and she instructed her representatives to observe a passive attitude.

The official opening of the conference at Constantinople was preceded by preliminary sessions from which the Turks were excluded: a proceeding naturally offensive to them, but necessary, as they could not well be permitted to take part in the discussion of what terms were to be imposed upon them. For once English and Russian diplomacy were in harmony. Lord Salisbury, the chief British representative, displayed a zeal for reform that was in rather surprising contrast to the recent attitude of the government he represented. He and Count Ignatiev worked hand in hand, with the result that the powers agreed upon a series of demands that were to be presented to the Turks. Mere promises of amelioration could no longer be accepted. Europe knew by this time that "the whole history of the Ottoman empire, since it was admitted into the European concert under the engagements of the Treaty of Paris, has proved that the Porte is unable to guarantee the execution of reforms in the provinces by Turkish officials, who accept them with reluctance, and neglect them with impunity." * The powers now insisted not only on local autonomy and improvement of administration, but also on the appointment of a foreign supervising commission to see that their decrees were carried out.

These unpalatable demands were presented to the Turks at the first 'full' meeting of the conference (December 23). But proceedings were soon interrupted by the sound of the booming of cannon. Whereupon Safet Pasha, Turkish foreign minister, informed his astonished hearers that they were listening to a salute fired

* Instructions of Lord Derby to Lord Salisbury, *Parliamentary Papers*, 1877, xci, Turkey, No. 2, p. 7.

in honor of the constitution which His Majesty, the Sultan, had just conferred upon the peoples under his rule. It was, indeed, deserving of a salute, for it was all that it should be, modern and democratic, granting not only representative government but full and equal rights to every race and creed in the transformed Ottoman state. Compared with what it bestowed, the reforms insisted upon by the powers looked insignificant enough; but as its blessings were for all, it made no mention of special autonomies, and, of course, foreign control was inconceivable.

The only immediate effect of this theatrical stroke was to irritate the members of the conference, who regarded the whole thing as a farce and continued to press their demands. On January 13, 1877, they presented them, with some modifications, as an ultimatum. But the Turks stuck to their ground, refusing to tolerate foreign interference and claiming that the Sultan had of his own free will conferred on his subjects, Christian as well as Mohammedan, far more than the powers had asked for. Even the solemn departure of all the ambassadors from Constantinople failed to affect their attitude of flat defiance. The Turks did not believe that Europe could or would do anything.

In this belief they were right as regarded Europe as a whole, but one power had gone too far to retreat. Genuine as was his reluctance at being drawn into war, Alexander II felt that his dignity and that of his country made it impossible for him to submit tamely to further rebuffs. He would have liked to act as the mandatory of Europe, but though the other powers had joined in diplomatic notes and had even withdrawn their representatives from Constantinople, they would go no further. Russia had to act alone, at her own risk and peril; and, above all, before launching herself upon the enterprise, she must take into account the attitude of Austria.

And that attitude by this time was clear enough. The government at Vienna not only was determined to take no action itself, but also had no intention of granting a free hand to its ally. Its position was a disagreeably strong one. The geographical situation of Austria on the flank of the Russian armies made it unsafe for them to venture into the Balkan Peninsula unless assured of her neutrality, and if the Tsar in his anger should turn them first against her, not only would she have the probable help of England, but she could at the last resort count on the protection of Germany. It was all very well for Bismarck to declare, as he did in his celebrated speech to the Reichstag of December 5, 1876, that for Germany the whole Eastern Question was not worth the bones of one Pomeranian grenadier. He might proclaim her equal friendship for both her allies and her desire to maintain good relations between them. None the less, he had made his choice and let it be understood that in case of a conflict, if the integrity of Austria were threatened, Germany would take up arms in her behalf.* It is true this did not prevent him from continually repeating in public, and still more in his interviews with the Russian ambassador, the assurances of his warm friendship for Russia and his desire to serve her. He also, in these interviews, gave his advice in favor of a war with Turkey.†

The result of all this was that after some negotiation two Russo-Austrian agreements were concluded. The first, which was signed at Vienna on January 15, 1877, provided that, in case of war, Austria would observe an attitude of friendly neutrality and would give diplomatic support; but it was stipulated that though Serbia and Montenegro might render military aid, their territories must not

* He expressed himself definitely in this sense at a parliamentary dinner (December 1), and in accordance with his wishes, his words were widely quoted in the newspapers.

† Tatishchev, *Alexander II* (in Russian), ii, pp. 349–354.

be used by Russian troops as a base of operations. This meant, to use a term not then invented, that they were not to be regarded as in the Russian 'sphere of influence.' In a second agreement, not signed till three months later, but regarded as an integral part of the first and antedated accordingly, it was stipulated, as at Reichstadt, that in case of a dismemberment of the Ottoman empire, Serbia and Montenegro were, indeed, to obtain some enlargement, but that Austria should have Bosnia and Herzegovina, while Russia was to get back the part of Bessarabia she had been forced to cede in 1856.*

Once more Count Andrássy and his master had cause to feel satisfied and doubtless did so, even though Emperor Francis Joseph in a telegram to the Tsar

---

* Russia was also to have Batum and the adjacent territory, but by Gorchakov's express wish this was not mentioned in the compact, which had to do with the European and not the Asiatic territories of the Porte. Wertheimer, ii, p. 393.

expressed the fervent hope that these agreements might never have to be carried out and that their efforts to maintain peace might yet succeed. Alexander II, indeed, still hesitated.* The excited public urged him to action; but he and his ministers realized that Russia had not yet recovered from the wounds of the Crimean war. Her army was not thoroughly reorganized, her finances were in bad condition, even the emancipation of the serfs and the other great reforms of the earlier years of his reign had been followed after the first enthusiasm by disappointment and discontent, and there were already dangerous symptoms of revolutionary agitation. All these facts made the position of Alexander II and his chancellor a difficult one.

The Tsar accordingly made a last effort to bring about a peaceful solution. On March 31 a document was drawn up in

* The beginning of the winter was the worst season for the opening of military operations.

London embodying a final appeal to the Porte. The proposal for a foreign commission was dropped, and was replaced by a mere threat of further action in case the reforms demanded were not carried out. All the other powers adhered to this protocol, though without much enthusiasm, perhaps even without the wish that it should succeed. The situation was further complicated by what the Turks regarded as an unfair demand for their demobilization before that of Russia. At any rate, the Sultan, supported by the unanimous vote of the parliament he had summoned under the new constitution, had now determined to refuse all concessions. On April 10, 1877, the Porte answered the powers in a circular note in which it refused to tolerate any foreign interference in its internal affairs, and three days later it notified Montenegro that the existing armistice had come to an end. On April 24 Russia declared war.

The position of Russia at the outbreak of hostilities was not particularly favorable from either a political or a military standpoint. By considerable sacrifices she had secured for the time being the neutrality of Austria, but that neutrality was in no true sense friendly, and it was provisional, dependent on the highly uncertain course of events. From the British came the word "that the decision of the Russian government is not one which can have their concurrence or approval,"* and Lord Derby gave formal warning against the inclusion of Egypt or the Suez Canal in the sphere of hostilities, or the occupation of Constantinople, or any change in the treaties of 1856. The attitude of Germany was one of ostentatious disinterestedness, that is to say, lack of interest. France and Italy did not need to be taken into serious consideration.

On paper, at least, the army Russia could put into the field was much larger

* *Parliamentary Papers*, 1877, xci, Turkey, No. 18, p. 4.

than that of her adversary, and, thanks
to the introduction of railways, it could
be conveyed to the front with far greater
ease than in any of her previous wars.
That front, however, was a contracted
one, owing to the agreement with Austria
which precluded the use of Serbian territory for military purposes. Russia, too,
had not since regaining her liberty of action by the Treaty of London of 1871 had
time to rebuild a Black Sea fleet capable
of meeting the entire Turkish navy, which
could be concentrated against it. She
was, therefore, unable to bring troops and
supplies by water or to hamper the Turks
in this respect. The only way in which
she could reach the European territory of
her foe was through a Turkish vassal
state, the principality of Rumania.

Rumania had to make up her mind as
to what would be the wisest policy to
pursue under the circumstances. Russia
had repeatedly invaded the principality
in former wars, and had even occupied

it for years at a time, and had now no thought of allowing her sole passageway to the Balkan Peninsula to be barred by any desire of Rumania for neutrality. Attempts at resistance on her part would be hopeless, even with Turkish aid, and would bring her misfortune; mere passive acquiescence offered only negative advantages; but actual collaboration with Russia promised the much desired boon of complete emancipation from Turkish sovereignty. She therefore decided to conclude a treaty providing for the free passage of Russian troops, and when the Turks resented this as an act of hostility and bombarded Rumanian forts across the Danube, she declared war on her own account. Difficulties about subordination, however, as well as the Russian contempt for the untried Rumanian militia, and disinclination to share with them the glory of the campaign, resulted in their not taking part at first in military operations.

In the spring of 1877 the military reputation of the Turks did not stand high. For the last two hundred years they had been defeated by inferior numbers in almost every important battle they had fought—not only by Europeans, but even, not long before, by the unwarlike Egyptians. The glories of their earlier triumphs had thus become much dimmed. It was known that they were brave and could defend fortifications obstinately, but their discipline was loose, their officers were ill trained, and the progressive disorganization of the Ottoman empire in the last twenty years did not promise well for the efficiency of the troops. The Russians accordingly were confident of rapid and easy success, and they made the mistake of undertaking their campaigns in both Europe and Asia with insufficient forces. Such ventures have often been justified by the outcome and might well have been in this case, but when such risks are run a single check may lead to grave disaster.

The campaign began brilliantly. With little difficulty the Russians succeeded in crossing the Danube, they rapidly over-ran much of northern Bulgaria, seized some of the Balkan passes, and made a daring raid beyond. But the Turks, who in history have more than once surprised the world both favorably and unfavor-ably, rallied in an unexpected manner. A small Russian force incautiously attacked a much larger Turkish one under Osman Pasha in an important strategic position at Plevna and was shattered. When more men had been hastily gathered and the onslaught was renewed ten days later, the result was a second and more serious defeat. For a time the situation was critical, as the Turks now took the offensive and the Russian armies were in danger of being thrown back shamefully across the Danube. In Asia, too, they presently met with a sharp check and had to retreat to within their own frontiers. In both fields weeks must elapse before considerable reënforcements could be brought up.

Under these circumstances the Russians, putting their pride in their pockets, appealed to Rumania for aid. This was granted on terms highly honorable to the Rumanians, and, assisted by the lack of capacity shown by the Turkish generals, saved the situation. The Russian and Rumanian forces did, indeed, fail in a third assault on Plevna, one of the great battles of the nineteenth century; but they kept their ground, and on the arrival of fresh troops they turned the attack into a siege. The Turks held out through the autumn, till at last, on December 10, Osman Pasha, after a fierce belated attempt to cut his way through, surrendered his army.

After this events followed each other swiftly. The Russians, heedless of the rigors of a winter campaign in the mountains, gave their disorganized enemies no respite, and forced their way across the Balkans, routed the Turks in one engagement after another, and pressed on toward Constantinople. The tide had also turned in Asia, where the Turks were defeated in battle and the fortress of Kars was taken by storm. Serbia now joined in the war, and Greece was stirring.

European diplomacy, which had been waiting on the course of military events, now awoke to feverish activity. Austria and Great Britain, in particular, were resolved not to accept any solution disadvantageous to their interests. They asserted that the status of the Eastern Question was part of the public law of Europe, as established by the Congress of Paris in 1856, supplemented by the conference in London in 1871, and that no changes could be made in it without the consent of all the signatories. They wished, indeed, to be consulted by Russia in advance, that is to say, to have a voice in the negotiations.

As the foreign offices at Vienna and London held much the same views, they kept in close touch with one another. London would have liked to take common action, and proposed this as early as May 20, 1877. Andrássy, however, suspected the British government of having in mind the exigencies of home politics and of desiring his aid in order to obtain a diplomatic and parliamentary triumph for its own selfish benefit.* He did not wish to alienate too completely the Slavs in the Balkan Peninsula, and to make them feel that Russia was their only friend. Moreover, the relations of Austria with Russia were not the same as those of England. Great Britain and Russia were still at peace with one another and maintained correct official intercourse, but that was about all. There was no pretense of cordiality between them, and one disagreeable act more or less meant little. But Austria was theoretically an ally of Russia and did not wish to give unnecessary offence. Besides, unknown to London,

* Wertheimer, iii, p. 28.

Andrássy had in reserve his agreement of January 15, which, if it were carried out, as he meant that it should be, would safeguard Austrian interests. It was better to wait and to watch the course of events, while not neglecting precautions for the future. He therefore declined all English suggestions of immediate alliance, and proposed instead a secret interchange of declarations by which the two powers bound themselves to uniform but separate diplomatic, and, if need be in the future, to joint military action.*

To this suggestion the English agreed. For many reasons they were anxious to see the war brought to an end as soon as possible. While deeply disliking and distrusting Russia and determined to oppose her advance, they did feel a certain sympathy for the Christians under Turkish rule and for their aspirations, whereas Austria's foreign policy has seldom been affected by such sentiments. The Eng-

* Wertheimer, iii, p. 39.

lish cabinet, moreover, was not united as
to what it should do, or just how far Russia should be allowed to go in weakening
the Ottoman empire. The prime minister himself, Lord Beaconsfield, who
throughout favored vigorous action, was
nevertheless disturbed by the fear, felt
likewise in France, that Bismarck rejoiced
in the whole Eastern complication and
wished to profit by it in order to attack
the French at a moment when they could
obtain no outside help. On one point the
English government was clear; under no
circumstances would it permit the Russians to get into the Mediterranean; that
is to say, it would not consent to any
change in the clauses of the Treaty of
Paris which closed the Straits to Russian
ships of war. For the same reason, it was
opposed to the creation of a strong Slavic
state, especially to one on both sides of
the Balkans and with a seaport on the
Ægean, for it believed that this state
would be a vassal of Russia, its creator.

Here Austria was equally determined. There must not be a Great Serbia or a Great Bulgaria that included Macedonia. Such a state, besides being a natural ally of Russia, would be a bar to the extension of Austrian influence to the southward, and might even serve as a centre of encouragement to discontented Slavic elements in the Dual Empire.

On the 8th of June, 1877, before her armies had even passed the Danube, Russia had informed England as to the conditions under which she would be willing to concede peace to the Turks, provided they asked for it before her troops had crossed the Balkans. These conditions, which in the main corresponded with those in the agreement with Austria, were not accepted by England as satisfactory, but the matter rested for a time. The disasters at Plevna made immediate discussion superfluous. But when at last Osman Pasha surrendered and the Russians swarmed across the mountains, capturing or driving before them without respite whatever was left of the Turkish armies, both Austria and England began to make pressing inquiries as to Russian intentions and to intimate that they themselves ought to be consulted.

The demand was most unwelcome. It often happens toward the close of a war that interested third parties not only proffer their good offices to bring hostilities to an end, but even insist that they have the right to be heard regarding the terms of peace. Such intervention may be hailed by the defeated combatant, but the victorious one fears and dislikes it and rejects it if he can. In 1871 Bismarck had been worried over the danger that some other nation might try to meddle in the peace negotiations between Germany and France. In 1878 the Russians had special reasons for resenting any attempt to rob them of the fruits of success. They believed that they had done alone what had been the duty of all Europe, and yet they had been refused assistance or even a mandate from the other powers, though all had made the same demands and had met with the same rebuffs. The war had proved more difficult than the Russians had expected; they had suffered heavy losses of men and money; they had met with severe reverses and some humiliations; and now that they had finally triumphed, they were not disposed to let those who should have helped, but had only hampered them, dictate what terms of peace they might impose on the enemy. The Russian public knew nothing of any secret agreement with Austria, and the Russian army, after what it had gone through and had achieved, was as anxious to enter Constantinople in triumph as the German one had been to enter Paris in 1871. Tsar Alexander II, in the correspondence which he still maintained with Emperor Francis Joseph, while asserting that Russia would act according to the spirit of the agreement of

January 15, declared that after all that
had happened it could not be carried out
to the letter.   On January 26, 1878, the
Russians officially informed Vienna of the
demands which five days later they imposed on the Turks by the armistice of
Adrianople.

By this time the Turks were no longer
in a position to haggle over terms, but
Austria and England were, and had no
thought of allowing themselves to be
brushed aside.   On February 3, Andrássy,
in a circular note, invited the powers to
an international conference at Vienna.
Russia, though agreeing to the idea, objected to Vienna as a meeting place, and
it was decided to hold, not a conference,
but a formal congress of the powers at
Berlin.   The international situation was
alarming.   On January 28 the English
ministry had asked Parliament for an
additional military grant of six million
pounds.   Five days earlier the British fleet
had been ordered to pass the Darda-

nelles. The order had been recalled, but on February 7 it was repeated and was carried out. The Russians answered by declaring that if the English entered the Bosphorus, they themselves would occupy Constantinople. The forces of the two nations were now almost in sight of one another, and any step forward on the part of either would have led to immediate war. The Balkan Peninsula was in a state of wild confusion. The Bulgarians had begun to take sanguinary revenge on their enemies for the outrages they had suffered, and the Mohammedans retaliated when strong enough to do so. A Greek army invaded Thessaly, only to be withdrawn at the urgent remonstrance of the powers, and the promise that the interests of Greece should be looked after at the general settlement. Meanwhile the Russians, undeterred by the preparations against them and by the forthcoming congress, continued their negotiations with the representatives of the Sultan, till on March 3 they concluded the Peace of San Stefano.

By the terms of this treaty Russia was to receive a war indemnity of 1,410,000,-000 roubles, an uncertain asset in view of the state of Turkish finances; but 1,100,-000,000 of it were to be commuted for the district of the Dobrudja in eastern Bulgaria, and for a territory in Asia including the fortress of Kars, the port of Batum, and the town of Bayazid. Rumania was to obtain her independence, but was to cede Bessarabia to Russia and receive the Dobrudja in exchange. Serbia and Montenegro were to have independence and an accession of territory. Bosnia and Herzegovina were to get reform and autonomy. Most important of all was the creation of a large Bulgarian vassal principality, extending to the Ægean and to the frontiers of Albania. Until it was organized it was to be occupied by Russian troops, for as long as two years if necessary.

The news of this treaty excited loud clamors. Mohammedans in Bulgaria, Greeks, Rumanians, and even Serbians protested violently. These outcries Russia could disregard, but not the opposition of England, who now refused to attend the proposed congress unless the whole San Stefano agreement should be submitted to it for discussion and modification. On April 1 Lord Salisbury, who had succeeded Lord Derby as foreign secretary, sent a circular note to the powers, sharply criticising the treaty. Military preparations were feverishly pushed. Lord Beaconsfield startled Europe by the despatch of Indian troops to Malta, as an indication that in case of hostilities Britain could count on the resources not only of the United Kingdom but of her whole vast empire—a foretaste of what she was to do on a much larger scale a generation later. Andrássy, on his part, made no secret of his opposition to the terms of peace as they stood, and called on the

Austro-Hungarian delegations for an extra military credit of 60,000,000 gulden.

The government of Tsar Alexander II now found itself in just the position it had feared from the beginning, but had not succeeded in avoiding. Its victorious armies stretched as far as the gates of Constantinople, but their flanks and rear were at the mercy of an Austrian attack; and whereas Russia could not count on an ally, Austria would be joined by England, and also by Rumania, who was intensely exasperated at seeing the aid she had furnished at a critical moment requited by a demand for a cession of her territory. Worst of all was the patent fact that Bismarck stood behind Austria. He had encouraged the policy of Andrássy from the start; indeed, he has been accused of having suggested it; this is probably an exaggeration, but it is easy to understand why he should have wished to turn the energies and ambitions of Austria to the eastward, and even have looked upon her, up to a certain point, as the German advance guard in that part of the world. None could say when he would think the time had come for the formidable intervention of Germany, an intervention that might have results for Russia far more disastrous than those of the Crimean war.

England by herself was less to be feared. She could hardly send aid sufficient to enable the Turks to prolong their resistance with success, and the Russians believed that from Central Asia they could make trouble for her in Afghanistan and India.* But her demands were so much like those of Austria that it was probable that if either state took up arms it would have the support of the other. The conflict that had just ended had proved unexpectedly costly in blood

* Skobelev, the most brilliant Russian general, and one with Asiatic experience, had made a plan for the invasion of India which he believed feasible. It was at this time that the Russian mission was sent to Kabul which alarmed England and led to the second Afghan war.

and treasure, Russia was exhausted, her finances were in bad shape, and her victorious army near Constantinople was melting away by disease, while before its eyes the city, at first almost undefended, was being provided with fortifications which grew more formidable with every week that passed. Rage as the Russian government and people might, the perils of a general war were too great for them to face, except at the last extremity. To avoid disaster they must come to some sort of terms with their rivals.

Bismarck, with his usual common sense, had insisted that the Congress of Berlin should not meet until all serious points in dispute had been settled by preliminary agreement. Gradually this was accomplished. Though England yielded more than had been expected at St. Petersburg, most of the concessions were made by Russia, who by three secret compacts, signed in London on May 30, gave up her creation of a Great Bulgaria, but kept Bessarabia in Europe and Batum and Kars (but not Bayazid) in Asia.

But while the British government was reducing the gains of Russia, it was also providing itself with securities for the future. By the Cyprus Convention,* signed June 4, it guaranteed to the Turks from Russian aggression the rest of their possessions in Asia, in return for which the Porte undertook "to introduce necessary reforms, to be agreed upon later between the two powers, into the government, and for the protection of the Christian and other subjects of the Porte in these territories." And in order that Great Britain might the more easily defend and protect these territories (the Turks knew nothing of the Anglo-Russian arrangement signed five days before), she was to receive the island of Cyprus to occupy and administer. Having thus sanctioned in her own case the principle of

* Also called the Convention of Constantinople. *Parliamentary Papers*, 1878, lxxxii, Turkey, no. 36, pp. 3, 4.

appropriating Turkish lands for the good of the Ottoman empire, she was in a position to advocate it in the case of her friends, and two days later, in one more secret agreement, she promised to support the views of Austria in regard to Bosnia and Herzegovina.

After the main difficulties had been surmounted in advance, the representatives of Europe could meet with the expectation of a happy result from their labors. The celebrated Congress of Berlin was a gathering of very distinguished and able men, Beaconsfield, Gorchakov, Andrássy, Salisbury, and various minor lights, presided over with masterful vigor and tact by Prince Bismarck, then at the full height of his genius and his fame. He had hoped that the proceedings would last but a few days, and would consist in the prompt ratification of the bargains made between the great powers, and in the submission to them by the smaller ones, whose representatives were only allowed to appear before the Congress, but not to take part in it. Yet in spite of the ruthless energy with which Bismarck pushed matters through, the Congress lasted for a month (June 13 to July 13), and there were several disagreeable and even critical moments before everything was settled. The Bulgarian question, as the most difficult, was taken up first, and some time passed before every one was agreed as to just what boundaries and rights should be assigned to the three parts into which the Great Bulgaria of San Stefano was to be divided: namely, a vassal Bulgarian principality, an autonomous province of Eastern Rumelia, and a Macedonia. This last was handed back to the tender mercies of the Turks, with no protection except promises of reforms that were never to be carried out, and that did not preserve it from another thirty years of constantly increasing oppression and misery. On the other hand, the Turks had a painful surprise when by previous arrangement their friend, Great Britain, proposed that Bosnia and Herzegovina should be handed over to their other friend, Austria. When they attempted to object they were browbeaten by Bismarck and freely lectured on the dangers of obstinacy. Russia, bound by her agreements, was unable to do anything, and the Turks, left unsupported, yielded in the end. It was voted that Austria should occupy and administer the two provinces, and should also occupy the district of Novibazar. The Rumanians protested in vain at being obliged to cede Bessarabia. They met with some sympathy but no aid. Serbia and Montenegro were granted accessions of territory, and Montenegro, thanks to Russian insistence, was to have a seaport on the Adriatic, though without the right of policing its waters, which was put in Austrian hands. The Russians obtained Kars and Batum, but had to declare an intention of making Batum a free port. Their war indemnity of 300,000,000 roubles was left to them, but as it was stipulated that this should have no precedence over other Turkish debts, the prospect that it would ever be paid was remote.

Shortly before the Congress came to a close, it was astonished, the Russian delegates most disagreeably so, by the announcement of the Cyprus Convention. Other territorial changes were suggested in private discussion, but got no further. Various minor matters were attended to, including a vague promise of a rectification of boundary for the Greeks and of reforms for the Armenians, and a stipulation that whatever was left of the decrees of the Congress of Paris and of the London Conference should be still regarded as binding. The members of the high assembly then departed to their homes, among them Lord Beaconsfield, who on his return proclaimed to an admiring throng that he had brought back 'peace with honor.'

CHAPTER III

The Congress of Berlin in 1878 marks one of the turning points in the history of the Eastern Question. The changes in the map made or consecrated there were almost revolutionary in their extent. In 1856, at the Congress of Paris, the powers had attempted to rejuvenate and to fortify the Ottoman empire. They had freed it from the Russian menace, they had guaranteed its integrity, they had renounced the right of interference in its internal affairs, and they had expressed kindly approval of its projects of reform. It was the spoilt child of Europe. In 1878 it fared differently. Friends, enemies, former vassals, while squabbling with each other, were one and all ready to possess themselves of its territory. Its wishes were the last thing that any

one thought of consulting, and its promises imposed upon nobody. No wonder
that the Turks felt every man's hand to
be against them, and that, far from carrying out the mandates of the Congress in a
compliant and cheerful manner, they
adopted a policy of passive resistance,
which they pushed as far as they dared.
Nothing in the nature of reform was done
or even attempted for Macedonia or Ar-
menia; the Bosnian Mohammedans were
secretly instigated to resist Austrian occupation; the Albanians were played off
against the demands of Montenegro, until a joint naval demonstration of the
powers and the threat of other measures
finally brought the Porte to terms and to
the keeping of its promises. In the matter of the extension of the Greek boundary, Turkey, not unnaturally, showed no
inclination to grant anything. It was in
vain that the powers took up the matter
and decided she must yield Thessaly and
Epirus; she remained obstinate, till in the

end she wore down their insistence and managed by a final agreement, in 1880, to keep most of Epirus, to the wrath of the Greeks.

But the Turks were not the only people dissatisfied with the results of the Congress. The anger of the Russians was still hotter. They had fought what they believed was the fight of Europe and of humanity, they had shed their blood and spent their treasure without stint, and in the hour of victory their hand had been stayed, the other nations had combined against them, their fair compensation had been cut down, while their jealous rivals, Austria and England, had helped themselves to whatever Turkish lands were to their liking. At Berlin Russia had found herself without a friend. Even Germany, the ally who owed so much to her, had adopted an attitude of lofty neutrality, which was only a mask for her support of Austria.

Most of the smaller states were no

better pleased. The Bulgarians had, indeed, not a little to be thankful for when they compared their situation with what it had been two years earlier, but they had seen the brimming cup dashed from their lips. The Great Bulgaria of San Stefano had been partitioned, and much of it had been handed back more or less completely to the Turks. In consequence, the disappointment of the Bulgarians was intense. Far from resigning themselves to their new lot, they never gave up the hope of regaining what had once been promised to them, and the chief historical importance of the Bulgaria of San Stefano has been that it created for a nation an ideal they have pursued unswervingly ever since.

Serbia was now independent and enlarged, as was Montenegro, who had obtained her long-coveted seaport, but both these states bitterly resented the Austrian occupation of Bosnia and Herzegovina, which were inhabited by their kinsmen, and which they had desired for themselves. They also disliked the Austrian occupation of Novibazar, which separated them from one another. Greece was much dissatisfied with the smallness of her acquisitions, and she regarded the new Bulgaria as a dangerous rival for territory which she had long hoped might some day be hers. Altogether, the outlook for future harmony in the Balkans was not promising.

Even the two powers that had fared best could not, as later events have proved, look back on their success with complete satisfaction. Great Britain may have obtained 'peace with honor,' though not every one thought so, but she soon learned that she had been egregiously mistaken in her estimate of the future relations between the Russians and the Bulgarians, and she had cause to regret that she had opposed the creation of the Great Bulgaria, which would thereafter have given a different aspect to the history of the Balkan Peninsula, and would have saved Europe the perplexities and horrors of the Macedonian question. By the Cyprus Convention, England assumed a guarantee for the integrity of Asiatic Turkey. This, luckily for herself, she has never been called upon to make good, but she also assumed an obligation to protect the Armenians, an obligation that was to weigh heavily on her in after-times, and that she has found herself painfully unable to fulfil. With the Turks her relations soon underwent a radical change. After the fall of the Beaconsfield ministry in 1880 she ceased to be what she had been for the previous half century, the protector to whom they looked for aid in every crisis. At the head of the new Liberal government was Mr. Gladstone, the champion of oppressed peoples, the benefactor of Greece, the author of the famous pamphlet on *The Bulgarian Horrors*. Henceforth the voice of England was no longer that of a friend. The change was to prove lasting. From that day to this, Great Britain and the Ottoman empire have rarely been on cordial terms.

Even Austria-Hungary was by no means so content with her acquisitions as might have been expected. Count Andrássy had steered his course with skill and had brought his vessel of state triumphantly into port. He had checked the ambitions of Russia, he had prevented the creation of a powerful South Slav kingdom, he had kept open the road to Salonica, and he had secured for his sovereign a territory that might be regarded as a compensation for the loss of Lombardy and Venetia. Under his guidance Austria, excluded from Italy and Germany, had found a new field for her expansion, and she had entered into this heritage not by war and conquest, but in response to the official mandate of Europe, which had commissioned her to take over these lands from the Turks, who had shown themselves incapable of retaining them. And yet there were shadows to this picture. In Austria, and still more in Hungary, the two chief nationalities, the Germans and the Magyars, were none too well pleased at the strengthening of the Slav element in the Dual Empire, which sooner or later must result from the bringing of over a million more Slavs under the rule of Francis Joseph. At the last moment Andrássy had decided to get the right, not of 'annexation' of Bosnia and Herzegovina, but only of 'occupation and administration.' He was probably influenced by the difficulty as to the disposition of the two provinces between the two halves of the monarchy if they were formally annexed, and also by his anxiety to obtain the acquiescence of the Turks. If he had asked for outright annexation he might not have been able to obtain the signatures of their plenipotentiaries at Berlin, and without them his action would bear an appearance of violence which he was eager to avoid. Even as it was he had to agree to a secret promise, which we may feel sure he never intended to keep, that the occupation should be only temporary. Doubtless he thought that he was getting the substance and sacrificing only the shadow,* neverthe-less his imperial master and the military party at home seem to have been disap-pointed, and his resignation a few months later may have been connected with this. He was never restored to favor, a thing Bismarck declared to be incomprehen-sible in a country possessing so few states-men as Austria. The uncertainty as to the ultimate status of Bosnia and Herze-govina was destined to remain one of the disturbing elements in the Balkans for thirty years. When annexation was at last formally decreed, it almost led to a general conflict.

---

* In private he described the Austrian occupation of Bosnia as annexation "very badly disguised." H. Drummond Wolff, *Rambling Recollections*, ii, p. 194.

Andrássy had hoped and believed that the territories he had won for his master would submit peacefully to their new lot. Instead, the Mohammedan population rose in savage resistance, which was overcome only by the employment of large forces and after sharp fighting. The Christians accepted the change more quietly, for it brought them great benefits, but the largest element among them, the Orthodox Serbs, never renounced their nationalistic aspirations. On the contrary, as time went on, these aspirations grew constantly stronger. They rendered good relations between Austria and Serbia almost impossible, till they culminated, in 1914, in the tragedy of Seraievo, the immediate cause of the European war.

Germany, at the Congress of Berlin, had, according to Bismarck's well known phrase, played the part of 'the honest broker.' She had smoothed over the differences between the other countries and had approved of the division of the spoil between them, while asking nothing for herself. And yet, disinterested as Bismarck claimed to have been, and dexterous as his management certainly was, he had scant reason to look back on the events of the last few months with satisfaction. He had, it is true, helped to launch Austria on a career of expansion to the southeast in sharp rivalry with Russia, thereby insuring that the two would not combine against him, and securing himself against any return on the part of Austria to a policy of intervention in German affairs. This was well enough, but the League of the Three Emperors, the one that of all others he preferred, and the one that precluded most completely any combination of powers dangerous to Germany, was now, if still nominally in existence, a mere sham. What was more, he had failed in his attempt to aid Vienna without alienating St. Petersburg; and though he may have had confidence in the military strength of Germany as compared with that of her eastern neighbor, never in his long career did Bismarck regard the attitude of Russia as a matter of small importance. As between Austria and Russia he had deliberately chosen to support the former,* but without swerving from this policy he had sought to avoid arousing Russian susceptibilities, except from delight in annoying and humiliating Gorchakov or in occasional outbursts of temper. Speaking publicly, ten years later, he declared: "My conduct at the congress was such that I thought, after it was over: Well, if I had not got long ago the highest Russian order set in precious stones, I ought to get it now." † None the less, his effort to retain Russian friendship had resulted in failure. To the Russians his boasts of

---

* The reasons given by him in his memoirs may be accepted as far as they go.

† *Reden*, xii, p. 463.

what he had done for them appeared a mockery. No small services that he might have rendered them could obscure the fact that, from their point of view, Germany under his guidance had in the hour of need deserted the friend to whom she owed so much. And as the false friend arouses more bitterness than the open enemy, every one from the Tsar down resented the so-called neutrality of Germany as keenly as the open hostility of England or Austria.

For popular opinion Prince Bismarck, as a rule, cared little, especially for Russian opinion. He strove to win the good will of the emperor, not that of the nation, and he abominated the Panslavists, who repaid him in kind, but now the Tsar and his advisers were as angry as the most ardent Panslavist. During the winter of 1878–79 the newspapers of St. Petersburg and Moscow indulged in violent recriminations with those of Berlin, even mentioning with favor the idea of a Franco-

Russian alliance. In the reorganization
and redistribution of the Russian armies
that followed the war with Turkey, the
troops stationed in Poland were strengthened to an extent that excited alarm in
Germany, where this action was regarded
as a sign of ill will. On their side the
Russian government, and especially the
emperor, were irritated by what they believed to be the unfriendly attitude of the
German representatives in the international commission determining the boundaries of Bosnia.

The sincere admiration and affection
that the Tsar, a man of frank, impulsive
nature, had long felt for his aged uncle,
the Kaiser, and the many years of close
intimacy between the two, made his disappointment and resentment the more
keen. Was this the gratitude to which
he was entitled? Had not Emperor
William himself written in 1871: "Prussia
will never forget that she owes it to you
that the war did not assume the most ex-

treme dimensions.   May God bless you
for it." *   At last, unable to restrain his
feelings longer, Alexander II poured out
his grievances to the German ambassador
at St. Petersburg and ended with a warning, and a week later wrote to his imperial uncle a letter † complaining in a
tone almost of menace of the conduct of
Germany, which he ascribed chiefly to
Bismarck's resentment against Gorchakov.‡ There was more truth than tact

* *Politische Correspondenz Kaiser Wilhelm's I*, p. 302.

† He wrote at the same time a similar letter to Emperor
Francis Joseph, if we may trust Bismarck's statement to St.
Vallier. Chaudordy, *La France en 1889*, p. 261.

‡ "I understand perfectly that you are anxious to maintain
your good relations with Austria, but I do not understand
why it is to the interests of Germany to sacrifice those of
Russia. Is it worthy of a real statesman to put into the
scale a personal quarrel when it is a question of the interests
of two great states born to live on good terms with one
another and when one of them rendered the other, in 1870, a
service which according to your own words you said you
would never forget? I should not have presumed to remind
you of this, but the situation is becoming too serious for me
to conceal from you the fears that are harassing me of consequences that might be disastrous to our two countries. May
God preserve us from them and be your guide." H. Kohl,
Wegweiser durch Bismarck's Gedanken und Erinnerungen,
p. 170.

in his remarks, and the letter greatly
incensed Emperor William. Bismarck
profited by the opportunity. He had
just heard of the forthcoming resignation
of Andrássy, which had filled him with
alarm, as perhaps meaning the triumph
of clerical and anti-Prussian influences at
Vienna and a change in Austrian policy.
Although he had soon been reassured on
this point, he deeply regretted the retirement of a statesman whose aims had
accorded so well with his own. On
August 13 he had expressed by telegraph
a desire to see Count Andrássy again at
any time and place that was convenient
to him. Andrássy replied on the 15th
(the day that the letter of the Tsar was
written), fixing Gastein as the meeting
place.

A close alliance between Germany and
Austria was an idea which Bismarck had
entertained before and even informally
suggested. This may seem strange in one
who had risen to greatness by his reso-

lute anti-Austrian policy, which had triumphed in the war of 1866, and had led
to the aggrandizement of Prussia and to
the expulsion of Austria from the German
Confederation.   Yet, much as he had disliked the previous hollow friendship between Vienna and Berlin, which he believed to be entirely to the advantage of
the former, and convinced as he was that
Prussia could only fulfil her ambitions by
a successful war with Austria, none the
less, even before that war was finished, he
had begun to look forward to better relations in the future. The obstinacy with
which in the hour of victory he had
stood out against the eager wish of his
master and of the Prussian military
leaders for an acquisition of Austrian
territory, was due only in part to the
immediate dangers that he perceived in
case Prussia should show herself im-
moderate in her demands. It was also
due to his extraordinary foresight as to
the advantages of not alienating Austria

permanently, but of leaving the way open to a subsequent reconciliation. In the League of the Three Emperors, Bismarck had already reaped a first reward for this policy, and he was now to reap a further one when he believed the moment had come to guarantee Germany against the consequences of Russian resentment.

The friendship between Russia and Prussia was of old standing. For over a century, since the alliance concluded between Catherine II and Frederick the Great in 1764, the two countries, although at times there had been coolness between them, had never been at war with one another, except, nominally, during the Moscow campaign of Napoleon I. Their soldiers had fought side by side at the battle of Leipsic and on other glorious fields, they had entered Paris in triumph together, and Emperor William himself, then a boy, had taken part in that triumphant entry. Since then the two countries had often befriended each other to the advantage of both. The closely related courts of Berlin and St. Petersburg had been on intimate terms, and the sovereigns were bound together by sincere mutual affection. But such sentimental considerations did not weigh with Bismarck. Earlier in his career the friendship of Russia had brought him great benefits for which he had had to pay little in return. He was not disposed now to pay much and get little. If Russia had been willing to give him a free hand against France, his attitude might have been different, but as he later wrote in his memoirs: "That for Russian policy there is a limit beyond which the importance of France in Europe must not be decreased is explicable. That limit was reached, as I believe, at the Peace of Frankfort—a fact which in 1870 and 1871 was not so completely realized at St. Petersburg as five years later. I hardly think that during our war the Russian cabinet clearly foresaw that, when it was over, Russia would have as neighbor so strong and consolidated a Germany." * This was true, and whatever may have been Bismarck's designs in 1875, the famous war scare at least made clear that Russia was not minded to permit him to attack France.

Another consideration also weighed with him. He says later in his memoirs: "In point of material force I held a union with Russia to have the advantage," † and history has shown that this assumption was correct. On the other hand, Germany had great material force of her own, so great that in an alliance between her and Austria there could be little doubt as to which would be the dominant partner—as again later events have proved. With Russia there was no such prospect. To be sure, the time was past when St. Petersburg could take with Berlin the

* *Gedanken und Erinnerungen*, ii, p. 231.
† *Ibid.*, ii, p. 234.

superior tone used by Emperor Nicholas I toward his brother-in-law, King Frederick William IV. But even so, complete docility to German suggestions could hardly be expected on the banks of the Neva. Russia was too mighty, too proud, and too ambitious a state to remain long content with the rôle of second fiddle. She would wish to receive at least as much as she gave, especially as she believed there was a good balance due her already, and she would not be likely to alienate for long her own liberty of action. There was some ground for the fear Bismarck expressed to Shuvalov, "that if the German policy confined its possibilities to the Russian alliance, and, in accordance with the wishes of Russia, refused all other states, Germany would with regard to Russia be in an unequal position, because the geographical situation and the autocratic constitution of Russia make it easier for her to give up the alliance than it would be for us." *

* *Gedanken und Erinnerungen,* ii, p. 225.

This does not mean that under certain circumstances, and if paid his price, Bismarck might not have gone back to the policy of a close alliance with Russia, even, to a certain extent, at Austrian expense, and such a policy is probably what would have best pleased his sovereign. But neither Russia nor Germany was ready at the last analysis to grant the other a perfectly free hand as against France and Austria respectively. This explains the failure of the offers of Radowitz in 1875 and of Werder in the following year, and, on the other hand, the refusal of Bismarck to the Russian proposal for an offensive and defensive alliance, made to him in 1877 * and renewed and urged upon him a year later by Shuvalov, just before the Congress of Berlin.

To these considerations we may add the deeper one of the common nationality and history of the Germans in Germany and

---

* Tatishchev, *Alexander II*, ii, p. 487. See also *Gedanken und Erinnerungen*, ii, p. 220.

of those in Austria.   For a thousand years
they had been in the same empire, and
their present political severance from one
another dated back scarcely more than a
·decade.   Such factors weighed with Bismarck, and he mentions them among the
reasons for his decision, but we must not
exaggerate their importance.   Though he
was a German to the core and the chief
maker of German unity, he had little of
the spirit of intense nationalism so char-
acteristic of the next generation; he had
never belonged to the 'Great Germany'
party, and without a qualm he had cut
off ten million Austrian Germans from
their immemorial connections, just as he
never worried over the fate of the Germans in the Russian Baltic provinces.
His positive genius was far removed from
the dreams of the modern Pangermanist.
He neither rhapsodized over the merits
of *Kultur* nor looked forward to an inevitable conflict between Slav and Teuton,
though he regarded Russian Panslavism

as a menace. In short, he was a patriot, but not a nationalist, clear-sighted and practical rather than sentimental or imaginative. He had already shown by his conduct throughout the whole Eastern crisis that if the League of the Three Emperors should break down, and he were forced to choose between Austria and Russia, it was Austria he would support. Now, angered by the attitude of Russia since the Congress of Berlin, and fearing that in spite of assurances to the contrary the retirement of Andrássy might lead to a change of policy at Vienna, he determined while there was still time to bind Germany and Austria together by an alliance which should put an end to the dangers that threatened them both. Having, therefore, commented at length on the letter of the Tsar, in such a manner as to inflame rather than soothe the anger of his sovereign, and having submitted a draft for a stiff reply, he started for Gastein, eager to meet his Austrian

friend and to push matters to a conclusion.

Count Andrássy, on his part, if we may
trust to a memorandum that he wrote in
1888, had been aiming for just such a
result ever since he had become foreign
minister. It did not, therefore, take long
for the two statesmen to reach an understanding when they came together at
Gastein. They agreed that after each
had obtained the approval of his master,
Bismarck should proceed to Vienna to
enter into formal negotiations for an
Austro-German alliance. The idea was
immediately approved by Emperor
Francis Joseph, but the aged German
emperor was at first quite unfavorable
to it. Although offended at the tone of
his nephew, he still clung to the hered-
itary friendship between Berlin and St.
Petersburg, and he was just sending
General Manteuffel with a special mes-
sage to the Tsar. He also had not entirely got over his old distrust of Austria.

He telegraphed, accordingly, to Gastein, forbidding Bismarck's journey to Vienna, and only gave his consent after the most vigorous remonstrances on the part of the chancellor, who declared that his own position and further continuation in office would be impossible if he were to be disavowed in this manner. Emperor William yielded with reluctance, and presently, in answer to an invitation from Tsar Alexander, decided to meet him and clear up the situation. Unwelcome as such a step was to Bismarck at this juncture, he was unable to do anything, except submit to his master a long memorandum on the relations between Germany, Russia, and Austria, in the past, present, and future. The document, however, seems to have had little effect. On September 3, at the Russian frontier town of Alexandrovo, uncle and nephew greeted each other once more. All the clouds between them soon vanished.* The Tsar

---

* For an account of the meeting, see Tatishchev, *Alexander II*, ii, p. 550.

expressed his profound regret if anything he had written had offended his uncle, and declared that his feelings and purposes had been misunderstood in Germany. He brought forward his minister of war, General Miliutin, the man supposed to be the leader of the anti-German faction, to aver that there was no truth in the charge, and that the recent Russian military movements were not in any sense hostile. The two monarchs parted completely reconciled, and with Emperor William satisfied that his chancellor's suspicions of Russia were without real foundation. He therefore rejected flatly the idea of an Austro-German alliance directed against Russia, declaring that such an act would now be dishonorable and treacherous on his part.

This brought matters to a crisis. Bismarck, from Gastein, where he was kept by the state of his health, continued to assail his master with arguments and with threats of resignation. In answer the emperor talked of abdicating rather than stooping to a dishonorable act. Only after obstinate resistance did he unwillingly consent to negotiations for a defensive alliance, but it must not be one that was specifically directed against Russia.

On September 21 Prince Bismarck arrived in Vienna. He was well received. The discussions between him and Count Andrássy and the drawing up of the treaty lasted but three days. Andrássy declined Bismarck's suggestion that the pact should be made part of the constitution of both empires, thus bringing them into a permanent relation with one another that would recall in a measure the Germanic federation dissolved by the war of 1866. He also refused to sign any general treaty of alliance, declaring that Austria had no quarrel with France and wished to keep on good terms with her, partly out of consideration for England. As Germany was amply able to hold her own against France without assistance, just as Austria was against Italy, an alliance for such contingencies was not necessary or desirable. The only real menace was from Russia, or from a combination of Russia and some other power, and this was all that should be provided against. On this point we may suspect that Bismarck merely made a show of following the instructions given him. If he had cared at bottom, he would have displayed more vigor and obstinacy than he did in contesting Andrássy's arguments. As it was, he soon yielded to them, and in a memorandum to his emperor, on September 24, recommended the ratification of the agreement that had been reached.

This led to another acute crisis. Emperor William asserted repeatedly that the proposed treaty would be an act of ill faith on his part, after the assurances he had just interchanged with the Tsar. Again he talked of abdicating rather than consenting to such a thing. Why was not the best and simplest solution to admit Russia herself to the pact, and thus renew and strengthen the League of the Three Emperors? On the other hand, Bismarck once more came forward with the threat of his own resignation. He called to his assistance the chief men of the empire. He assured himself of the approval of the king of Bavaria, and he called on Prince Hohenlohe, the German ambassador in Paris, to add his arguments. Von Moltke brought the whole weight of his military authority and influence to bear on the same side. The crown prince also supported it with enthusiasm. The imperial ministers were unanimous in its favor, and announced their intention of resigning if the treaty were not ratified. Thus the aged emperor found himself alone. Most reluctantly he yielded to the pressure put upon him. The only concession that he was able to obtain was that though for the present

the terms of the pact were to remain
secret, he might in case of need inform
the Tsar of its scope.   To this Andrássy
consented, and on October 7, 1879, the
Austro-German alliance was signed by
him and by Prince Reuss, the German
ambassador in Vienna.

The news of what had been done soon
transpired.   In both Germany and Austria it was greeted with loud applause.
There were a few dissentients, especially
in Austria among the clericals and the
Slavs, but in the main both countries felt
that the alliance was a natural one,
founded on the interests of both, against
a common danger.   To the former partisans of Great Germany it seemed a partial realization of their once cherished
dreams, bringing together all Germans, if
not into one confederation, at least into
close and, they hoped, permanent partnership.   It threatened no one, for it was
purely defensive in character, but by its
existence and power it formed a dam

against the progress of Panslavism, while it helped to keep France quiet by making her feel her isolation.

In England, still under the Conservative and anti-Russian ministry of Lord Beaconsfield, the news was well received. Lord Salisbury, in a speech at Manchester on October 17, hailed it as "good tidings of great joy." In France, as was to be expected, it aroused apprehension. The French feared that Bismarck might now attack them without fear of the restraint which had been imposed upon him in 1875. He gave no indication, however, of any such design. While he was negotiating at Vienna, he had expressly sought out the French ambassador there and had spoken to him most reassuringly as to German intentions. Indeed, his attitude during and after the Congress of Berlin was more friendly than it had been for years.

There remained Russia. Even without knowing the exact contents of the

Austro-German treaty, the Russians realized that the alliance was directed against
them and resented it accordingly. But
the Tsar took the matter quietly. On
November 4 Emperor William wrote a
letter to his "dear Nephew and Friend,"
enclosing the preamble to the treaty as
a memorandum and explaining with obvious difficulty and confusion the reasons
for his action. He even went to the
length of declaring: "I like to say to
myself that you will judge the principles
embodied in this important act at their
true value, and that you will agree with
them as strengthening the League of
the Three Emperors, which since the year
1873 has rendered Europe such signal
services." Alexander II replied that he
was glad "that this political transaction
contains absolutely nothing contrary to
my wishes," and that "I like to see in
it the return to that perfect understanding between the three emperors which, as
you remark with so much truth, has ren-

dered the greatest services to Europe."* The words of the Tsar may have been tinged with irony, but he continued on good terms with his uncle until his own death by assassination on March 13, 1881.

This event had little immediate influence on the international situation. The new Tsar, Alexander III, was a man of limited education and with no great range of ideas, profoundly honest, slow, conservative, religious, not to say bigoted, with a high sense of his duties and of his position. He had come to the throne under the most tragic circumstances, and, after a short moment of hesitation, he resolutely set his face against liberalism, and reverted to the traditions of undiluted autocracy. With stern determination he stamped the revolutionary movement almost out of existence and followed a firm reactionary policy. In foreign affairs he was nationalistic, with none of the cosmopolitanism that had character-

* Kohl, *Wegweiser*, pp. 178–182.

ized his predecessors for the last century
and a half.   But little as he loved foreign
nations, he was a sincere lover of peace
and intent on preserving it, and by nature
he was adverse to adventure or to wanton
enterprise.   He established friendly relations with his great-uncle at Berlin, and
he, and still more his quiet, moderate,
and cautious foreign minister, M. de
Giers, were soon on an amicable footing
with Bismarck.   The tension with Austria also relaxed, as was shown by a secret
treaty signed in 1881,* according to
which, in return for Austrian consent to
a union of Bulgaria and Eastern Rumelia,
"si elle se faisait par la force des choses,"
Russia agreed that Austria might, when
she chose, convert her occupation of Bosnia and Herzegovina into actual annexation.

The difficulty Austria had experienced

* See the article on Kálnoky by Friedjung in the *Bio-
graphisches Jahrbuch*, March, 1909. See also *Denkwürdigkeiten des Fürsten Hohenlohe-Schillingsfürst*, ii, p. 311.

in pacifying these two provinces led her to postpone for nearly a year longer her occupation of Novibazar, which was carried out, this time without resistance, in September, 1879. She thus kept open her passage to the southward and inserted herself between Serbia and Montenegro. She now possessed almost irresistible means of pressure upon Serbia, an inland state whose commerce with western Europe must pass through her territories, and whose capital, Belgrade, could be reached across the river by Austrian guns and could be threatened with immediate attack.

Besides this, the Serbians had been angered by the fact that Russia had assigned to Bulgaria, at the Peace of San Stefano, lands they regarded as theirs and had also supported Bulgarian claims at Berlin.* Serbia got these lands

* On Serbia at the Congress of Berlin, see the article by Dr. Vladan Georgévitch in the *Revue d'Histoire Diplomatique*, 1891, pp. 483–552.

in the end * with the aid of Austria, who had opposed her expansion in other directions and to whose dictation she had to submit in railway and commercial affairs. Continuing her pressure, Austria next succeeded in winning over to her policy Prince (later King) Milan, a man of intelligence, but of untrustworthy character, who felt far from secure on his throne. In 1881 he brought back from Vienna the draft of a treaty which he persuaded his minister of foreign affairs to sign. It was then put away in the archives, and very few even of the prime ministers and ministers of foreign affairs of Serbia knew of its existence for the next dozen years, by which time it had come to be regarded as inoperative.

By this treaty of June 28, 1881,† in order to establish a "perfect friendship" between the two states, Serbia bound her-

* The territory about Pirot. Bulgarian claims extended as far as Nish.

† For an account of it, see the article by Stojan Protitch in the *Fortnightly Review* for May, 1909.

self not to tolerate any intrigues against
Austria-Hungary, who gave a reciprocal
assurance, promising also to support
the dynasty and to assist Serbia and
her interests with other European cab-
inets; Serbia in return undertook "not
to negotiate with or conclude political
treaties with any other states without
previous agreement with Austria-Hungary." The two powers promised each
other mutual friendship and neutrality in the event of war with a foreign
state. Even if this treaty did not mean
any great accession of strength to Austria, it helped to keep Serbia in the position of her client in Balkan affairs.

But strong and satisfactory as the Austro-German alliance was, it was capable of being improved or at least supplemented by the accession of another
power, and that power, after earlier hesitation and reluctance, was now eager to
be admitted into partnership.

The young kingdom of Italy had been

completed by the occupation of Rome in September, 1870. Unlike Prussia, Italy had not reached greatness by brilliant victories of her own; her success had been due not only to her efforts, but also to the misfortunes of others, which she had turned to good account. After the achievement of her unity, she still feared an Austrian attempt to reverse the verdict of 1859 and of 1866, and that this time she would not have a French or a Prussian ally. She feared still more that some power might take up the cause of the Pope and demand the restoration of his temporal authority, and she believed that the greatest danger in this respect threatened her from the side of France.

The relations between France and Italy extend over a period of more than two thousand five hundred years: that is to say, to the beginning of the known history of each. Even before the founding of Rome, Celtic tribes from Gaul had penetrated into the heart of the peninsula and settled there as conquerors. Rome itself was captured by the Gauls in 390 B. C., and as late as the time of Cæsar, though Cisalpine Gaul had long been under Roman rule, the frontier of Italy proper was not the Alps but the Apennines and the Rubicon. On the other hand, during the centuries that Gaul was part of the Roman possessions, it became so thoroughly Latinized that, like Spain, it retained its Latin character in spite of a period of barbarian conquest and domination. Only its eastern portion was permanently Germanized; in the rest of the land the intruders were soon absorbed. Therefore in this present age of nationalistic consciousness Frenchmen and Italians regard themselves as bound together by ties of blood, of identical cultural origin, and of common civilization and ideals. Questionable as these ties may be from a scientific point of view, the belief in them and the sentimental value attached to them are real. 'The sisterhood of the Latin nations,' to use a favorite term, represents the same sort of vague nationalistic ideals as Panslavism, Panteutonism, and other movements of the kind.

This feeling of sisterhood has not kept the Latin nations on especially good terms with one another in the past. Much as the French have owed not only to Roman but to Renaissance Italian culture, they have none the less invaded Italy again and again for frankly selfish reasons. Their first appearance as benefactors, though still as plunderers, was in the days of the French Revolution, when they brought in temporarily a certain measure of political liberty, long unknown south of the Alps. In the nineteenth century, liberals in France, as elsewhere, sympathized with Italian aspirations for freedom and political unity. Napoleon III, himself an Italian almost as much as a Frenchman, was moved by sentimental considerations as well as by calculation when he took up the Italian cause and declared war on Austria in 1859. His two victories of Magenta and Solferino soon led to the emancipation of nearly the whole peninsula (if not quite in the way he had intended), and though he had his hesitations and misgivings, and was not willing to abandon the Pope altogether, he remained to the end of his reign the sincere friend of Italy. By his attitude in 1866 he helped her to obtain Venice.

For all this the Italians were grateful to him and to France. They had, however, grievances which loomed large in their eyes. The Peace of Villafranca, by which Napoleon, in obedience to sound military and political considerations, halted his successful campaign and left Venice for some years longer in the hands of Austria, was a sad disappointment to the Italians, whose hopes had been inflamed by the emperor's ill-advised proclamation that he would free Italy "from the Alps to the Adriatic." It is true that he still gave them his support, and it would have been impossible for them to achieve their unity without his protection against Austrian interference, a protection to which they owed as much as to the genius of Cavour or to the enterprise of Garibaldi. But when their success went much further than he had foreseen, he had exacted, in compensation for his services and for the sacrifices of France, the cession of Nice and Savoy. Nice has in the past been at times connected with Italy, at times with France, and geographically belongs with either. The peasants in the country about speak a dialect of Provençal, but by 1860 the town of Nice had become Italianized, and it was here that Garibaldi was born. The duchy of Savoy is situated on the French side of the Alps and has never been Italian in language, but it was the home of the dynasty that had now been raised to the Italian throne, and as such was dear to them.

The enforced cession of these two districts, although not objected to by the inhabitants themselves, has not been forgiven by the Italians to this day. Whenever relations have been strained between Italy and France, the eyes of those who dream of Italia Irredenta—and every Italian patriot has dreamed of it more or less—have turned in the direction of Nice and Savoy, and of the island of Corsica, which once belonged to the republic of Genoa and has been French only since the middle of the eighteenth century.

Another cause of Italian discontent was the continued occupation of Rome by French troops, in deference to the wishes of the clerical party in France. When the garrison was withdrawn in 1867, Garibaldi's ill-advised expedition against the city led to its prompt return, and to the painful incident of the hero's defeat at Mentana. In 1870 Italy, if given permission to occupy Rome, was ready to join with France against Prussia, her partner of four years earlier. But as Napoleon refused his consent until too late, the Italians, without running any risks, profited by his disasters, and after the withdrawal of the French garrison seized the Eternal City.

Meanwhile in France there was much division of opinion. Many were enthusiastic for the liberation of Italy and proud of the part their country had taken in it, but the powerful clerical party condemned the policy of the emperor altogether and supported the territorial claims of the Pope. There were Frenchmen, too, who, though not clerical in their sympathies, yet could not shut their eyes to the fact that there were disadvantages in the creation on the southeastern frontier of France of a new great power and future rival in the Mediterranean, whose ambitions might some day conflict with hers. Granted that the aspirations of the Italians toward national unity were, like those of the Germans, legitimate in themselves, was it, after all, the business of France to further them from sentimental reasons when their success must diminish her own relative position among European states ?*

In the later part of the Franco-German war, a number of Italian volunteers served in the French army under Garibaldi, and though neither they nor their leader achieved much success, the sentiment that inspired their action was appreciated. But after the Peace of Frankfort the relations between France and Italy became worse. The Italians had grown weary of being reminded of a debt which they regarded as being by this time paid or cancelled, and indeed many of them, including King Victor Emmanuel, felt that they had owed gratitude to Napoleon III rather than to the people he had governed. They

* "Napoleon III said to me in Paris that he planned to make a powerful nation out of Italy. I replied, 'Your Majesty, that is a ward that may become stronger than his guardian.'" Poschinger, *Also sprach Bismarck*, iii, p. 151.

had little sympathy for the French republic, whose example might encourage the
republican party in Italy, though they
feared a Bourbon restoration, believing
that it would mean a French intervention
in behalf of the Pope. This fear was
strengthened by the outspoken advocacy
of the papal claims by many French
royalists, including the Pretender, the
Comte de Chambord himself, and also
by the fact that until October, 1874, the
French government unwisely kept a man-
of-war stationed at Civita Vecchia, the
port of Rome.

The Italians, therefore, began to look
for friends in other quarters. In 1873
King Victor Emmanuel visited Vienna
and Berlin, and there was talk of the
probable adhesion of Italy to the League
of the Three Emperors. But these first
advances led to nothing. The three empires looked askance at Italy and felt no
particular need of her friendship. Her
alliance with Prussia in 1866, although it

had been profitable to both parties, had
led to singularly little good feeling between them.   From first to last they had
mistrusted one another.   The Prussians
had a poor opinion of Italian military
capacity, and the Italians, although,
thanks to the successes of their ally,
they obtained Venice, were humiliated
by the course of the war and chagrined
at the treaty of peace.   Bismarck seems
to have entertained scant liking or respect for them;* from Austria they could
hardly expect cordiality, and Russia was
indifferent.

In 1877, aroused by rumors of the
agreement of Reichstadt, the Italian government sent Francesco Crispi on a mission to sound the German chancellor as
to the possibility of an alliance between
Italy and Germany against France and
Austria.†   But Bismarck, while express-

* In 1880 he remarked: "They are like carrion crows on
the battle-field, that let others provide their food."   Busch,
Bismarck, ii, p. 233.
† See Crispi's account of the mission in his memoirs.

ing a willingness to make a defensive treaty against France, frankly declared that he was on excellent terms with Austria and would remain so. In answer to Crispi's declaration that Italy could not permit Austria to have Bosnia and Herzegovina without compensation for herself, he suggested, not a rectification of her immediate frontier, which was what Crispi was doubtless hinting at, but that she should appropriate Turkish territory in Albania. Nothing came of this suggestion, and at the Congress of Berlin Italy neither gained anything herself nor dared oppose the gains of Austria. This outcome produced disappointment and discontent in the peninsula,* which was not much allayed by the statement of the ministry that "Italy had returned from the congress with clean hands"; others called it with empty hands. France, too,

---

* Crispi declared in a speech at Naples: "We were humiliated at Berlin as the last people in Europe; we returned slapped and despised." Chiala, *Pagine di storia contemporanea*, ii, p. 17.

came back from Berlin 'with clean hands,' but she had something in her pocket,* and that something was an object Italy coveted.

The Roman province of Africa has more than once played its part in history. From here the Punic city of Carthage established her rule over the shores of the western Mediterranean and sent her ships in the Atlantic as far as Britain and down the coasts of Africa. After her fall there rose on the same site a new Roman Carthage, long the second city in the West. Then came the Vandal and later the Arab conquest. Of Carthage few traces remain, but some miles away the city of Tunis had its periods of glory as the capital of various Mohammedan dynasties. In the sixteenth century it was fought over by the Spaniard and the Turk, and became the home of a piratical state, nominally vassal to the Ottoman empire. When the age of piracy came

* Words of Waddington on leaving the congress.

to an end, its fortunes declined, and by
the last quarter of the nineteenth century the regency of Tunis seemed almost
in a state of dissolution. The rule of its
sovereign, the Bey, was tyrannical and
corrupt; the treasury was empty; and
the first fatal step in outside interference,
foreign control of finance, had already
been taken. But the natural resources
of the country were as great as they had
been in its brightest days, the soil was
as fertile, the climate as mild as ever.
All that it needed to bring back its former
prosperity was enlightened government
and foreign capital and enterprise.

No acquisition overseas could be more
alluring to the Italians than Tunis.
Lying at their very door, it would as-
sure them the possession of the southern
as well as the northern sides of the nar-
row passage between the western and
the eastern halves of the Mediterranean,
that Mediterranean in which they regarded themselves as the heirs of the

imperial traditions of Rome. The natural conditions of the country were suitable for Italian colonization, and its small and backward population left plenty of land for the immigrants whom Italy's high birth rate enabled her to supply in any number desired, and who already formed much the largest foreign colony there. No wonder, then, that as soon as the kingdom of Italy was constituted,* and even before,† Italians began to talk of the necessity of bringing Carthage once more under the rule of Rome.

But if Italy's desire for Tunis was natural and legitimate, that of France was equally so. Half a century had now elapsed since the French, by the capture of Algiers, had set foot in North Africa.

---

* Mazzini wrote in 1871: "As Morocco turns toward the Iberian Peninsula and Algeria toward France, Tunis, the key to the central Mediterranean, linked in formation with Sardinia and Sicily and distant but some twenty-five leagues from Sicily, obviously turns toward Italy. . . . To-day the French are making eyes at it and will soon possess it, if we do not." *Scritti*, xvi, pp. 153, 154.

† For instance, in the writings of Gioberti.

In the course of time, after years of arduous fighting and enormous expense, with many hesitations and mistakes but with stubborn persistence, they had built up a colony that was just beginning to flourish. The possession of Algeria not only strengthened France in the Mediterranean; it also furnished her with compensation for what she had lost in Europe, as well as for the colonies of which she had been deprived in the previous century. Although the French settlers in Algeria were and always will be a minority of the population, they can give it their civilization and perhaps in time their language, making it, if not an African France, at least a fresh field for the expression of French character and genius, one distant less than a day's sail from the mother country, and capable of being united to it by strong and permanent ties. Algeria itself, however, is only the central portion of a region known a century ago as the Barbary states, the whole of which belongs naturally in the same hands, for it has the same general features and is inhabited by the same peoples. Geographically it has a well defined unity of its own. Its political divisions have been the result not of natural formation but of historical accident.

As soon as the French began to feel at home in Algeria they inevitably turned their eyes toward their neighbors east and west, the regency of Tunis and the empire of Morocco, the two other portions of this North African region.* Both were in such condition that they bade fair sooner or later to come under the control of some European power. Napoleon III, in his dreamy idealism, may have deemed that France should content herself with Algeria and should leave Tunis to Italy and Morocco to Spain. Other and more practical Frenchmen felt that if ever the

---

* Tripoli, though counted as one of the Barbary states, is separated from Tunis by the desert, which here reaches the coast.

time should come when these natural
prolongations of Algeria must fall into
foreign hands, those hands must be
French.   From every point of view—political, commercial, military—for Algeria
to have as a direct neighbor the territory
of another great European power would
be disastrous, no matter how friendly
that power might be. This was particularly true as regarded Tunis, which on
the map goes as obviously with Algeria
as does Portugal with Spain, or Sicily
with Italy.   In consequence, France
strove, on the whole with success, to
establish a preponderating influence in
Tunis, and she emphatically refused to
recognize the claims which the Sultan
of Turkey still put forth to suzerainty
there.

At the court of the Bey, as at many
other African and Asiatic posts, the chief
opponent to the French consul was
usually the British one.   After 1860
the Italian consul appeared on the scene

as a new and active force. Here as elsewhere the Franco-German war greatly
diminished French prestige and influence;
indeed, during its course an Italian expedition against Tunis was at one time
threatened.

When in 1878 the plan of the Congress
of Berlin was broached, it was at first
doubtful whether France would be represented. The contrast between her situation then and the one she had held at the
last European congress, that of Paris in
1856 after the Crimean war, was ex-
tremely painful to Frenchmen. To attend, and at Berlin of all places, seemed a
humiliation, but not to attend was for
France to abdicate her right to be consulted as a great power. She therefore
accepted the invitation, but on the condition that there should be no discussion
of Egypt or of the French protectorate
of the Holy Places. To this the other
powers readily assented: a detail which
did not, it appears, prevent Bismarck

from suggesting to England the occupation of Egypt.*

Toward the end of the congress, when M. Waddington, the French foreign minister and first plenipotentiary, was informed of the convention handing over Cyprus to England, he was so angered that he thought of leaving at once, thus probably disrupting the congress. Lord Salisbury sought him out and assured him that Great Britain, recognizing that the situation of France in the Mediterranean and as the possessor of Algeria gave her a right to shape the destinies of Tunis, would make no opposition when the time came for her to assert that right. M. Waddington was also given to understand, though just how has never been revealed, that Germany would have no

* In his communication announcing the Cyprus Convention, Lord Salisbury wrote to M. Waddington, on July 6, 1878: "I am telling Your Excellency no secret when I say that we have been very earnestly pressed, by advisers of no mean authority, to occupy Egypt—or at least to take the borders of the Suez Canal." Lord Newton, *Lord Lyons*, ii, p. 149.

objection to the acquisition of Tunis by France.*

This attitude on the part of both England and Germany was somewhat extraordinary. In 1830 England was so bitterly opposed to the French expedition to Algiers that she almost went to war to prevent it, and for many years after she viewed the presence of the French in North Africa with intense dislike. For her now, without solicitation, to offer Tunis to France was a startling reversal of policy. We may surmise that it was due chiefly to the fact that Tunis seemed to be destined to fall soon into the hands of some European power, and that England, who just then happened to be on quite cordial terms with France, and since 1870 no longer feared her as of old, was willing to grant her this compensation for the strengthening of the English position in the Mediterranean

* See G. Hanotaux, *Histoire de la France contemporaine*, iv, p. 388, n.

farther to the eastward. It is true that
England was likewise on excellent terms
with Italy, but if Italy should get possession of Tunis, she would hold both
sides of the Mediterranean at its nar-
rowest part, and might some day control
or at least menace the security of a
passageway which was of more importance to Great Britain than the Suez
Canal itself. From the point of view
of British interests, it was better that
the two sides should not be in the hands
of the same power, even if that power
were Italy.

The attitude of Prince Bismarck was
determined by a different set of considerations, which again we can only surmise,
as we lack direct evidence on the subject.
In 1873 Count Arnim, the German ambassador to Paris, said abruptly to the
Duc Decazes: "I forbid you to take
Tunis." * There was no good reason

* *Denkwürdigkeiten des Fürsten Hohenlohe-Schillingsfürst,* ii,
p. 199.

that we know of for the threat at that time. Arnim may have gone beyond his instructions, as he did more than once, or his menace may have been part of the policy of bullying which Bismarck then followed in much of his dealings with France. He cared little for the affairs of the Mediterranean, and he had no sentimental predilections as between France and Italy; but it was clear to him that if either of the two obtained the supremacy in Tunis, there would be an estrangement between them, and that this would accrue to the advantage of Germany.* If Italy had been willing from the first to court his favor and pay his price, he might perhaps have been willing to support her claims. Indirect overtures were

* Sir Charles Dilke, one of the best informed students of foreign politics in his day, and under-secretary for foreign affairs in the Gladstone cabinet of 1880, later wrote: "It at least seems plain . . . that a great deal of offering of other people's property took place, and that some of those offers were suggested by Prince Bismarck. In one case, at least, the same thing was offered to two parties, which is an ingenious method of inducing complications which may lead to war."—*Present Position of European Politics,* pp. 27, 28.

made to her by Austria and Germany
at the Congress of Berlin, but were rejected by Count Corti, who believed
that they were only intended to embroil
his country with France, and who had
been enjoined by his government to
adopt an attitude of reserve.* It is
worthy of note that not long before,
when Crispi was seeking for a German
alliance, Bismarck had suggested to him
the taking of Turkish territories on the
Adriatic, but had made no mention of
Tunis. He may have believed that Italy,
even if assured of support, would not
summon up the resolution to follow his
advice at the cost of French enmity. He
may also have believed that, if he could
launch France into a career of colonial
expansion, he would not only turn her
thoughts from Alsace-Lorraine and a war
of revenge, but also weaken her by divert-
ing her resources from her tasks in Eu-

* J. Grabinski, *M. Depretis*, pp. 255–257. See also the
appendix by Hans F. Helmolt in Arthur Singer's *Geschichte
des Dreibundes*, p. 253.

rope. Be that as it may, he let M. Waddington know that he would not stand in
France's way in Tunisian affairs, and in
the years that followed he maintained a
consistently favorable attitude.*

The temptation thus offered to France
was considerable, and possibly her statesmen were mistaken in not yielding to it
at once. But French public opinion was
hardly ready yet; the war of 1870 was
still too recent, the need of rest and recuperation still too pressing. There was
suspicion of Italian designs and intrigues,
but there was little inclination to take any
adventurous step in order to anticipate
them. Besides, anything Bismarck approved of was feared as perhaps concealing a trap. The government at Paris,
therefore, decided against immediate action, but Waddington, after his return,
took care to put on record, in a more
precise and perhaps exaggerated form,

* There are many indications of this in Hohenlohe, Busch,
and elsewhere. Bismarck was probably also pleased by the
reserve France displayed toward certain advances on the part
of Russia.

his conversation with Lord Salisbury, and
then to submit the paper at London and
thereby obtain a formal acknowledgment
that in substance at least his statement
was correct.

In Italy the results of the Congress of
Berlin were received with dissatisfaction.
Russia, Austria, England, and the Balkan
states had all obtained something, and
there were rumors of a concession to
France, whereas Italy had come out
empty-handed—and she had got rather
into the habit of expecting to profit from
each international crisis. Public opinion
in the peninsula was discontented and
restless. There was a renewal of Irredent-
ist agitation, which put a strain upon the
relations between Italy and Austria and
led to a threatening concentration of
Austrian troops on the frontier. In
Tunis, just as the English consul, Mr.
Woods, for twenty years the tireless
opponent of French influence, was re-
tired, a new and active Italian one, Sr.

Maccio, appeared on the scene in a ship-of-war and was installed with military pomp. He immediately plunged into a struggle with his equally active French rival, M. Roustan, and for a couple of years the duel between them continued, the Bey hearkening sometimes to the one and sometimes to the other,* while the country fell into ever greater confusion. In France and Italy the public followed the course of these events with increasing attention, and violent articles in the press heightened the irritation on both sides.

In all this the Italians were following a dangerous policy. As the weaker nation of the two, it was for their interest to bide their time and maintain the status quo, not to push matters to an issue. Instead, they angered and alarmed the French by their noisy activity, until the

---

* Roustan, in obedience to orders from Paris, was trying to persuade the Bey into signing a treaty that would make him a protégé of France. See C. de Freycinet, *Souvenirs: 1878–1893*, p. 168.

government in Paris, secure in its greater
strength and in its knowledge that Italy
would get no outside assistance, determined to settle the matter once and
for all. Taking as its pretext the viola-
tion of Algerian territory by an unruly
Tunisian tribe called the Kroumirs, it
despatched a punitive military expedition of 30,000 men. On April 24, 1881,
the French armies crossed the Tunisian
frontier, and without opposition pushed
on to the capital. On May 12, in the
palace of the Bardo,* the Bey was forced
to sign a treaty, which, while preserving
for him the semblance of sovereignty over
his subjects, deprived him of all real authority, and turned Tunis into a French
protectorate.

In preparing and carrying out this expedition, the ministry of Jules Ferry, then
in power in Paris, had shown itself calm
and resolute. It had not, however, been
frank in its explanations to the chamber

* Or Kasr-el-Said.

of deputies, nor scrupulous as to truth
in its preliminary assurances to Italy. It
also made the mistake of withdrawing a
large part of the army of occupation too
soon, and thus giving an opportunity for
an insurrection, which broke out and ne-
cessitated the sending of fresh forces and
some little fighting before it was sup-
pressed. Nevertheless, in spite of their
mistakes, Jules Ferry and his colleagues
deserved well of their country. They
gained for France a territory which has
greatly strengthened her position in North
Africa, and is without question one of
the most valuable of all her possessions.
Its progress has been steady and satisfactory; it has been admirably governed
from the first, and it presents perhaps
the most successful example of French
colonial administration. But it cost
France the enmity of Italy for twenty
years, and the entrance of Italy into an
alliance against her which lasted for a
generation.

The expedition against Tunis and the treaty of the Bardo aroused the Italians to frantic protest. Turn where they would, they could find no ally—except, perhaps, the Turks, who wished to assert the Sultan's suzerainty by despatching ships to the scene of action, but were stopped by the categorical declaration of the French that a Turkish fleet would be treated as an enemy. The great powers remained deaf to Italian appeals. In England public opinion was somewhat excited, but the hands of the Liberal government were tied by the benevolent assurances of its Conservative predecessor. Germany and Austria remained ostentatiously indifferent; Russia was more indifferent still. There was no help for the Italians. France was not to be stopped except by actual force, and they were too weak unaided to risk the arbitrament of the sword.

Throughout the peninsula the resentment was bitter. The Cairoli ministry, which had been in power, fell after the treaty of the Bardo, a victim to public indignation. Italy regarded herself as injured and humiliated, and she chafed at her isolation and weakness. She believed that France had cruelly wronged her, and her ill-feeling was heightened by a riot, accompanied by loss of life, between Italians and Frenchmen at Marseilles. She had relied in vain on assistance from England. When she turned to Germany and made fresh approaches for an alliance, she was met with the frank answer that the way to Berlin lay through Vienna.

To Vienna the Italians went accordingly. As a first step, King Humbert himself made a visit there at the end of October, 1881, despite the fact that Emperor Francis Joseph, on account of his relations with the papacy, had never been willing to return in Rome the visit King Victor Emmanuel had paid him at his capital in 1873. King Humbert was

received with friendly courtesy, but political discussion was avoided. In December the Italian foreign office instructed
its ambassadors in Berlin and Vienna to
begin negotiations for a definite treaty.
At both places their overtures were received with a calmness that was dis-
couraging. The truth was that though
the members of the Austro-German alliance perceived the advantages of admitting a new partner to their society, they
neither trusted nor greatly respected their
future friend, and they felt that they were
in a position to wait for advances and to
make their own terms. Prince Bismarck
graciously admitted that he was "satisfied" with the attitude of Italy,* and in-
timated that though he did not think the
time had yet come for an alliance between
her and Germany, he should be glad to
see her reach an agreement with Austria.
Cheered by this approval, the government
at Rome continued its negotiations with

* Chiala, iii, p. 282.

Vienna, which, however, progressed but slowly, as the views of the two parties differed in various respects. Several notes had to be interchanged, and Bismarck presently joined in and shared the discussion.

Italy asked for two things: first, a guarantee of the integrity of her territory, which should put an end to all danger of foreign intervention in behalf of the papacy; and, second, support for her position and ambitions in the Mediterranean. The first demand meant for Emperor Francis Joseph and for Catholic Austria a sacrifice of sentiment. It was a painful thing for them to consecrate the possession of Rome by the upstart house of Savoy. At last they consented to this, chiefly because the provision for a territorial guarantee, being mutual, bound the Italian government to set its face in future against the cry of Italia Irredenta. Germany, on her part, cared nothing for the territorial claims of the Pope, and had naturally no objections to a provision that offered her one more security for her possession of Alsace-Lorraine.

The second Italian demand was refused by both Berlin and Vienna. Neither had any interest in Italian ambitions in the Mediterranean or inclination to put themselves out to serve them. The French occupation of Tunis did not disturb them, and Austria at least was hostile to any extension of Italian influence in the Adriatic. All that Italy could get was a vague general promise that the allies would support each other within the limits of their own interests; and it was provided, to reassure Austria, that the principle of the status quo should be maintained in the Balkans. The *casus fœderis* for military support was only to become operative when one of the allies was attacked by two foreign powers. The duration of the treaty was set at five years, and it was to be kept secret.

During the course of the discussions

Bismarck had decided to conclude an identical treaty between Germany and Italy, leaving out only the clause in regard to the Balkans, which was of no interest to him. On May 22, 1882, the two documents which together constituted the Triple Alliance were signed in Vienna, the one by Count Kálnoky, foreign minister for the Dual Empire, and by the Italian ambassador, the other by the German and Italian ambassadors. Several months elapsed before the rumors as to the existence of the agreement were fully confirmed and it was officially admitted to the world.*

The formation of the Triple Alliance was another triumph for Bismarck. He paid almost nothing for it, as he refused to interest himself in Italy's Mediterra-

* For these negotiations, see Chiala, iii, and Fraknói, "Zur Entstehungsgeschichte des Dreibundsvertrags," in the *Deutsche Revue*, December, 1915. For a sharp criticism of the ambiguities in the text as at present known, see Fraknói, "Kritik des Dreibundsvertrags," *Deutsche Revue*, January, 1916.

nean affairs, and the guarantee he gave
of the integrity of her territory imposed
no burden upon Germany.   What he obtained was an important addition to the
forces of the Austro-German alliance in
case of a conflict with France and Russia.
To be sure, his opinion of the Italian army
was not high, but that it should menace
the French and not the Austrian frontier
in case of hostilities counted for a great
deal.*   The Italians had also a navy that
was reckoned as the third in Europe, and
could be of service to Germany, whose
fleet was still inferior to that of France.
Austria, too, in return for a considerable
profit sacrificed but little, for she had
definitely abandoned the idea of regaining
her lost Italian territories, though she was
determined to retain those she still pos-

---

* "That is what Prince Bismarck meant when he once
remarked that it was sufficient for him that an Italian cor-
poral with the Italian flag and a drummer beside him should
array themselves against the West, i. e., France, and not
against the East, i. e., Austria." Bülow, *Imperial Germany*,
p. 60.   See also Poschinger, *Also sprach Bismarck*, iii, p. 151.

sessed. The Triple Alliance relieved her from anxiety on that score and assured her against the possibility, which she had sometimes feared, of a league between Russia and Italy.

For Italy the advantage of the compact was more problematical, even though it was she who had solicited it, and though it was generally approved throughout the peninsula. In its favor could be urged that it put an end to the isolation that had weighed upon her, and that it made her feel she was being treated as a really great power. It avenged her for the humiliation that had been inflicted upon her by France, and it assured her against French attack in the future. It also secured her against Austria, and here we have one of the peculiarities of the situation. So deep-seated, in spite of what was loudly said to the contrary, were the causes of hostility between Austria and Italy, that many Italians believed that the only way for the two countries to remain at peace with one another was by becoming allies. Otherwise they must be foes. Finally, the friendship of Germany and Austria meant for Italy at least their benevolent neutrality if she should launch into colonial enterprises, and perhaps their support, if France were to interfere with her.

But critics of the alliance then, and still more later, asserted that most of these advantages were imaginary, since they were an insurance against perils that did not exist. Granting that France had made use of her superior strength to seize an object that had been coveted with good reason by both countries, there was no cause for believing that she meditated further aggression.* The French republic was becoming increasingly radical and anti-clerical, as was proved by its just having passed a set of school laws that had excited intense anger among good

* The Italian fears of French designs against Tripoli never had any justification.

Catholics. To imagine that it or any statesman serving it would undertake a crusade to restore the temporal authority of the Pope was preposterous. If Italy was isolated, so were Great Britain and Spain and many other powers, and they found themselves none the worse for it. If her policy was wise and she paid proper attention to her army and navy, she was strong enough not only to defend herself against any likely attack but also to make her aid well worth courting by other powers. Instead, by joining the Triple Alliance she had tied her hands in the choice of her friendships, sacrificing that of France for many years to come. It was useless to declare that the Triple Alliance was purely defensive, a league of peace to which none could properly object. No rhetoric could alter the fact that while France had shed her blood for the liberation of Italy, now Italy, in so far as she was able, had guaranteed to Germany the possession of Alsace-Lorraine. There was nothing for France to do but to accept the situation,* but her resentment was deep and lasting. This, however, did not trouble the Italians. They had found new friends and were content with them. For better or for worse, the Triple Alliance was destined to last for a whole generation, during which it was to be one of the dominant forces in the European world.

* For an excellent and dignified article on the subject, see G. Valbert, "Un publiciste allemand et son plaidoyer en faveur de la triple alliance," in the *Revue des deux mondes*, 1 June, 1892, pp. 683–694.

APPENDIX

I

THE AUSTRO–GERMAN ALLIANCE

The exact terms of the Austro-German alliance were known only to a very few people until they were officially published on February 3, 1888. There may have been supplementary conventions at different times, but there is no reason for thinking that any changes have been made in the original text.[1]

Inasmuch as their Majesties the German Emperor, King of Prussia, and the Emperor of Austria, King of Hungary, must consider it their inalienable duty to provide for the security of their Empires and the peace of their subjects, under all circumstances;

Inasmuch as the two Sovereigns, as was the case under the former existing Treaty, will be enabled by the close union of the two Empires to fulfil this duty more easily and more efficaciously;

Inasmuch as, finally, an intimate coöperation of Germany and Austria-Hungary can menace no one, but is rather calculated to consolidate the peace of Europe on the terms established by the stipulations of Berlin;

[1] Published in the Berlin *Official Gazette*, February 3, 1883. Translation in *British and Foreign State Papers*, lxxiii (London, 1889), pp. 270–272.

Their Majesties the Emperor of Germany, and the Emperor of Austria, King of Hungary, while most solemnly promising never to allow their purely defensive Agreement to develop an aggressive tendency in any direction, have determined to conclude an alliance of peace and mutual defence. . . .

ARTICLE I. Should, contrary to their hope, and against the loyal desire of the two High Contracting Parties, one of the two Empires be attacked by Russia, the High Contracting Parties are bound to come to the assistance one of the other with the whole war strength of their Empires, and accordingly only to conclude peace together and upon mutual agreement.

ARTICLE II. Should one of the High Contracting Parties be attacked by another Power, the other High Contracting Party binds itself hereby, not only not to support the aggressor against its high ally, but to observe at least a benevolent neutral attitude toward its fellow Contracting Party.

Should, however, in such a case the attacking Power be supported by Russia, either by an active coöperation or by military measures which constitute a menace to the Party attacked, then the obligation stipulated in Article I of this Treaty, for mutual assistance with the whole fighting force becomes equally operative, and the conduct of the war by the two High Contracting Parties shall in this case also be in common until the conclusion of a common peace.

ARTICLE III. This Treaty shall, in conformity with its peaceful character, and to avoid any misinterpretations, be kept secret by the two High Contracting Parties, and only be communicated to a third Power upon a joint understanding between the two Parties, and according to the terms of a special Agreement.

The two High Contracting Parties venture to hope, after the sentiments expressed by the Emperor Alexander at the meeting at Alexandrovo, that the armaments of Russia will not in reality prove to be menacing to them, and have on that account no reason for making a communication; should, however, this hope, contrary to their expectation, prove to be erroneous, the two High Contracting Parties would consider it their loyal obligation to let the Emperor Alexander know, at least confidentially, that they must consider an attack on either of them as directed against both.

In virtue of which the Plenipotentiaries have signed this Treaty and affixed their seals.

VIENNA, October 7, 1879.

                  (L.S.)   H. VII, P. REUSS.
                  (L.S.)   ANDRÁSSY.

II

THE TRIPLE ALLIANCE

The terms of the Triple Alliance have never been published, but Articles I, III, IV, and VII are given in the Austrian Red Book, issued in 1915.[1] The last part of Article VII, which refers to possible territorial changes in the East, and the meaning of which was the chief subject of dispute in the negotiations that preceded the

[1] *Diplomatic Documents concerning the Relations of Austria-Hungary with Italy*, pp. 179, 189, 190.

outbreak of hostilities between Austria and Italy, was not in the original treaty. It was inserted in 1887, when the treaty was renewed for the first time. The first part, on the other hand, may well have been in the original treaty, as we know there was a provision to this effect. Articles I, III, and IV were probably in the treaty of 1882; but the wording for III and IV cannot have been quite the same, because, as stated above, the original Triple Alliance was formed by the Austro-German treaty of 1879, supplemented in 1882 by separate though similar treaties between Italy and Austria, and Italy and Germany. In 1887 there was but one document, signed by all the parties to the treaty.

ARTICLE I. The High contracting Parties mutually promise peace and friendship, and shall not enter into any alliance or engagement directed against any one of their respective States.

They bind themselves to proceed to negotiations on such political and economic questions of a general nature as may arise; and, moreover, promise their mutual support within the scope of their own interests.

ARTICLE III. If one or two of the High Contracting Parties should be attacked without direct provocation on their part, and be engaged in war with two or several Great Powers not signatory to this Treaty, the *casus fœderis* shall apply simultaneously to all the High Contracting Parties.

ARTICLE IV. In the event that a Great Power not signatory to this Treaty should menace the safety of the States of one of the High contracting Parties, and that the menaced Party should be forced to make war on that Power, the two others bind themselves to observe toward their ally a benevolent neutrality. Each one of them in that case reserves to herself the right to participate in the war, if she should consider it appropriate to make common cause with her ally.

ARTICLE VII. Austria-Hungary and Italy, being desirous solely that the territorial status quo in the near East be maintained as much as possible, pledge themselves to exert their influence to prevent all territorial modification which may prove detrimental to one or the other of the Powers signatory to this Treaty. To that end they shall communicate to one another all such information as may be suitable for their mutual enlightenment, concerning their own dispositions as well as those of other Powers.

Should, however, the status quo in the regions of the Balkans, or of the Turkish coasts and islands in the Adriatic and Ægean Seas, in the course of events become impossible; and should Austria-Hungary or Italy be placed under the necessity, either by the action of a third Power or otherwise, to modify that status quo by a temporary or permanent occupation on their part, such occupation shall take place only after a previous agreement has been made between the two Powers, based on the principle of reciprocal compensation for all advantages, territorial or otherwise, which either of them may obtain beyond the present status quo, a compensation which shall satisfy the legitimate interests and aspirations of both Parties.

INDEX